Lonnie + Shirley

S0-ACQ-929

Make Life Count!

50
Ways To

Julie Alexander

Make Life Count!

50
Ways To

GREAT DAYS

Julie Alexander

Copyright © MM

All rights reserved.

No part of this book may be used or reproduced
in any manner whatsoever without the written
permission of the author and the publisher.

Printed in the United States of America.

Cover design and text layout by
Ad Graphics, Inc., Tulsa, Oklahoma.

Library of Congress Catalog Number: 00-091082

ISBN: 0-9659310-1-3

"Make Life Count! 50 Ways to Great Days" is a trademark of Great Days Presentations, Great Days Press, and Julie Alexander, denoting a series of products that may include but is not limited to books, audio cassettes, video tapes, and a variety of other products.

Published by:

Great Days Press
a subsidiary of Great Days Presentations
2002 Shari Lane
Garland, TX 75043

Other books by Julie Alexander:
Great Days: 50 Ways to Add Energy, Enthusiasm, & Enjoyment to Your Life

Order Information
To order copies of this book or to receive information on programs or other products by Julie Alexander, contact:

Great Days Presentations
toll free (877) GR8-DAYS
or visit our web site
www.JulieAlexander.com

A little help from my friends...

Ray Kroc, the founder of McDonald's said, "No one succeeds alone," and this book is the result of the efforts and support of many people.

Special "thanks" go to:

Ken and Ben Alexander for encouraging me to get started and to keep going,

Adam Alexander, Jo Anna Couch, Kathleen Fawcett, Kristie Dance, and Lonnie Hitchcock for their focus on the "little things" that make a big difference,

Barb and Jim Weems at Ad Graphics, Tulsa, OK for their professionalism and expertise,

Shirley Garrett, Robin Thompson, and Barb Wingfield – "The B.K.B." – who hold my feet to the fire on a daily basis,

My precious friends who encourage and support me in untold ways,

The readers and audiences who give me the privilege of delivering my message,

And the people who so willingly shared their stories with me so that I could share them with you.

Dedication

This book is dedicated to
my husband, Ken,
whose love, patience, support,
sense of humor, and quiet strength
provide me with an
abundance of great days.

Contents

Introduction

When I wrote my first book – *Great Days: 50 Ways to Add Energy, Enthusiasm, & Enjoyment to Your Life* – I had no idea that it would impact not only my life but also the lives of others in such a significant way. The response was overwhelming. For me, that book opened doors that would have never been opened otherwise, and it provided me with a way to reach people with a simple but heart-felt message.

The positive response from the thousands of people who read the book and shared it with friends and family made me realize that people in this hurry-up, competitive, time-compressed world are hungry for a few words of encouragement. We're all looking for a little bit of hope, a reminder of things we really already know, and the realization that we do, indeed, determine our own happiness.

The universal appeal of the book took me by surprise. *Great Days* was read by people of diverse cultures as well as diverse economic and educational backgrounds. Readers ranged in age from nine to ninety-nine. Secretaries, parents, students, executives, salespeople, engineers, laborers, teachers, health care professionals, lawyers, grandparents, newly-weds, physicians, high-tech specialists, social workers, grocery store clerks, fast-food restaurant employees, and bankers all related to its down-to-earth message. They all seemed to need some ideas for having great days themselves, or they knew someone who needed some help in creating great days. In fact, here are fifty comments from people who told me how they personally benefited from the book or how they shared it with others.

1. "I gave it to my teenager who needed some encouragement."

2. "I use it every week to motivate my sales team at our Monday morning meetings."

3. "I gave copies to all my friends for their birthdays."

4. "It's a great stocking stuffer! At Christmas, everyone in my family got their own gift of *Great Days.*"

5. "Our PTA gave books to all our teachers. They really need great days."

6. "I gave it to my uncle who was recovering from surgery."

7. "It made me feel better. It was just what I needed."

8. "I keep it beside my bed. When I can't sleep, I read a few chapters, and I drop right off!"

9. I sent a copy to my sister who was struggling through a difficult divorce."

10. "I left it in my doctor's waiting room for other patients to read."

11. "My 12-year-old wrote a book report on it."

12. "I read it to my grandmother."

13. "I used it in my Sunday school class."

14. "We put it in the library at our school."

15. "I gave it to a friend who had lost her husband."

16. "We gave the book to all our employees. We want them to have great days on and off the job."

17. "We put it in the gift shop at our hospital."

18. "I bought it for my son and daughter-in-law."

19. "Julie, I think of you every day. I keep your book in my bathroom!"

20. "I recommend it to all my patients."

21. "I use *Great Days* as part of my daily quiet time."

22. "My company gave copies to all our clients."

23. "I use it with my high school English class. The students write their own version of *Great Days*."

24. "I love the quotes!"

25. "Chapter 15 is my favorite!" (Chapter 15 – Eat Something Chocolate!)

26. "I sent it to my friend in Canada."

27. "I gave it to my mom."

28. "My brother, who lives in Great Britain, loved it. Everyone needs 'great days' no matter where they are."

29. "I shared it with my preacher."

30. "I gave it to my sorority sister."
31. "I gave it to my wife / husband."
32. "I bought it for my boss."
33. "I gave it to my secretary."
34. "I love the stories."
35. "It made a difference."
36. "You're right about the chocolate!"
37. "*Great Days* helped me through a tough time."
38. "It made me appreciate my great days."
39. "The book made me aware of how I can help others have great days."
40. "It was warm and inspiring."
41. "I didn't want it to end."
42. "It gave me great ideas for having great days."
43. "I carry it in my purse. It's a very large purse!"
44. "I've read it several times."
45. "It made me laugh."
46. "It made me think."
47. "It touched my heart."
48. "It's down-to-earth."
49. "It just makes sense!"
50. "It made me want more great days!"

That's really the bottom line. We all want more great days, don't we? We all want to be happy, and we want to make life count.

Now, here's the exciting part. You <u>can</u> have more great days in your life! You can be more purposeful in your living. You start by just deciding that you're going to make every day a great one. It's up to you.

And you've taken the first step. Maybe this little book can assist you in your quest for more great days. I hope you'll find it helpful, encouraging, inspiring, fun...whatever you need it to be, however you choose to use it. Maybe it will even help you sleep!

My wish for you is that you will live each day to the fullest, that you will make your life count. May you discover the joy, fun, peace, and purpose in the precious daily gift of life.

Wishing you great days,

Julie Alexander

About the author...

Julie Alexander works with organizations that want to boost morale and people who want to make every day a great one. Her motivating, informative presentations focus on cooperation, attitude, responsibility, and enthusiasm – the four cornerstones for daily success on and off the job.

A resident of the Dallas area, Julie is a graduate of Texas Christian University and holds a master's degree from Southern Methodist University. Her background includes experience in business, teaching, and television.

A recognized professional in her industry, Julie is a professional member of the National Speakers Association and past president of National Speakers Association/North Texas chapter. She is the recipient of NSA/North Texas' highest honor, the Joseph J. Charbonneau Award. This award recognizes excellence and professionalism in the speaking industry. In her personal life, Julie is married, is the mother of two grown sons, and is a proud mother-in-law.

If you'd like to have Julie speak to your organization, contact her at Great Days Presentations – toll free (877) GR8-DAYS or visit the web site www.JulieAlexander.com.

Make Life Count!

1

Focus.

"Who begins too much accomplishes little."
German proverb

*"At the moment one definitely commits oneself,
then providence moves, too."*
Goethe

When Theodore Roosevelt became the 26th President of the United States, he was the youngest President to date. In addition to the challenges of being the Chief Executive, Roosevelt was the father of six children. The most demanding was his eldest daughter, Alice, who was seventeen at the time that he took office. Alice was a handful. A rebellious, out-spoken, difficult young woman, she required a great deal of attention. Her behavior caused her father to comment, only partially in jest, "I can be President of the United States, or I can deal with Alice. I can't do both." Roosevelt was smart enough to realize that he couldn't do everything that was being required of him. And neither can you or I.

One of the biggest mistakes we make, one that causes us tremendous stress and frustration, is our lack of focus. We are pulled in dozens of directions all at the same time. We go here and there, and wind up nowhere, because we fail to focus our attention on our priorities. Like butterflies, we flit from one project to another, doing this and that, and at the end of the day, we feel as if we haven't accomplished anything significant. And sure enough, we haven't. We've wasted our time on small, often trivial, things and never gotten around to doing the big things that could really make a difference in our lives and the lives of others.

A business coach taught me a process that has helped me to stay focused, and maybe it can help you, too. Every day list three things that you want to accomplish. Of course, most of us do a lot more than three, but the discipline of writing down three high-priority items and then doing them is powerful. It's an exercise in focusing and becoming aware of how you're using your time and energy. It forces you to concentrate and to make a commitment to a limited number of tasks. And if you follow through, the sense of accomplishment is extremely satisfying. At the end of the day, you can say, "This is what I focused on today. This is what I did that made a difference in my life, my career, my family."

What are you focusing on today? Is it valuable? Is it positive? Is it a productive, worthwhile use of your time and energy? At the end of the day, will you feel good about what you've accomplished? Will you have a sense of satisfaction? Or will you feel frustrated, disappointed, maybe a little angry with yourself for frittering away the precious, irreplaceable minutes of your day? Focusing on the significant and learning to do the important things first will go a long way in helping you make life count.

2

Be a Positive Presence.

*"A happy person is not a person
in a certain set of circumstances,
but rather one with a certain
set of attitudes."*
Hugh Downs

His name was Virgil Calvin Hitchcock. (I've often wondered what his mother must have been thinking when she selected that name.) But his friends called him "Chuck." He was born in a rural community in Collin County, Texas, the second of six boys. A young man during the Depression, he held a number of jobs. He worked in a hardware store, drove a truck, worked as a milkman, ran a gas station, and dreamed of owning his own business, a dream that wasn't fulfilled until after his retirement from working for a utility company for thirty-three years. At the age of 34, he married Lonnie Mae Hight. And seven years after their marriage, they had a daughter – me.

Since I was not only his only child but also a child born when he was past forty, I was the light of his life, and he made me feel special. He believed in me, and since I valued his opinion on everything, I believed in me, too.

My dad was truly a "positive presence" not only in our home – where my mother and I were blessed by his smile, his loving spirit, and his sense of humor – but also at his job, at our church, and in our community. Although he had little formal education, he was, nonetheless, a wise man, and one who realized the value of relationships in both business and life. He was warm, friendly, outgoing – a person who sincerely cared about people. He could – and would – talk to anyone, and people liked him, because he was genuinely interested in every person he met.

My dad never had much money, but he counted among his friends the rich and the powerful, and they were honored to have him as a friend. His friends also included the poor and the downtrodden. They knew that they could count on Chuck to help them pay an overdue bill or provide a little grocery money to cover them until payday. He often denied himself in order to help someone in need or to contribute to a worthy cause.

My mother would frequently say, "I'm a rich woman." And she was, because she had a husband who adored her, a husband who was gentle and patient, who never raised his voice to her, who danced her around the kitchen, who showered her with love and affection and called her "Sweet." Riches aren't always found in bank accounts.

And I, too, was rich, because I was fortunate enough to have a daddy who loved me unconditionally and who taught me that cheerfulness is a choice and that attitude is everything.

When it comes to my positive upbringing, I want to keep in mind what I like to call "the breadcrumb" factor. In the fairy tale of Hansel and Gretel, the children dropped breadcrumbs as they walked through the forest so that they could remember where they came from. I, too, want to remember where I came from and to honor my parents by letting their lives shine through me.

My dad was truly a living example of a "positive presence," one of those people who – by just being himself – made wherever he was a little better and a little brighter. He made life count and made every day a great one.

Make Life Count!

3

Believe in Yourself.

"I think I can, I think I can, I think I can..."
<u>The Little Engine That Could</u>

*"It's not what you are that holds you back;
it's what you think you're not."*
Dr. Denis Waitley

*"No one can make you feel inferior
without your consent."*
Eleanor Roosevelt

*"The greatest pleasure in life is doing
what people say you cannot do."*
Walter Bagehot

*"It is difficult to make a man miserable
while he feels he is worthy of himself and
claims kindred to the great God who made him."*
Abraham Lincoln

*"I have never met a man who has given me as
much trouble as I have given myself."*
Dwight L. Moody

> *"I'm not offended by all the dumb blond jokes,*
> *because I know I'm not dumb,*
> *and I know I'm not blond."*
> Dolly Parton

What is it about us human beings? We have the tendency to look at other people and to think that they're prettier, smarter, happier, luckier, stronger, braver, richer, healthier, cuter, and funnier than we are. We think that other people are more popular, more intelligent, more athletic, more talented, more powerful, and more successful than we could possibly be. We think that other people have more "stuff" and that their "stuff" is better than our "stuff." We think others are far more capable than we are of accomplishing great things. We sell ourselves short. Believing in the abilities of others is far easier than believing in ourselves and our own talents and abilities. It's been said that all people hover on the edge of self-doubt. I would agree.

Lurking within many of us is a little gremlin called Self-Doubt. When we begin to consider stepping out of our comfort zone, trying something new, something different, something challenging, the Self-Doubt Gremlin begins to question us.

"Just who do you think you are?" "What makes you think you can do that?" "Remember those times when you tried things that didn't work?" "Remember all the failures you've had?" "What makes you think that you're _____ (fill in the blank with your own word or words – "intelligent," "brave," "talented," "rich," "pretty," "savvy," "strong," etc.) enough to do this?" "Don't you know that you're too _____(fill in the blank again – "old," "young," "dumb," "cowardly," "boring," "unattractive," "weak," "poor," "uneducated," "unknown," "inexperienced," etc.) to make this work?" "Haven't you figured out that you don't deserve success?"

The Self-Doubt Gremlin is a tough interrogator. His questions can stab at the very heart of our being and cause us to back away from opportunities or from trying anything new. We're afraid that the gremlin might be right, and if we should try and fail, we would only prove him so.

Before I wrote my first book, I had a lot of self-doubt. My family, my friends, my colleagues had been encouraging me to do it for a long time, but I was listening to the gremlin, and his haunting, persistent questions were louder than the positive words of support that I was getting from the outside.

One day I went to a meeting to hear a speaker whom I admire. She was talking about the book she'd written and about the difference it had made in her career and in her life. Someone in the audience stood up to ask a question. "Leslie," he said, "what did you say to all the nay-sayers in your life? What did you say to those people who doubted your ability to be a successful author?"

The speaker stood perfectly still as she carefully pondered the question. After a long, thoughtful pause, she said, "As I look back on it, the only nay-sayers I had were in my own mind."

I knew at that moment that she had verbalized for me what I had really known all along but couldn't confront. I knew that my nay-sayers were all inside my head. It was at that moment that I understood the destructive power of the gremlin and the role he had been playing in my failure to believe in myself. And I also knew that I – and I alone – had the power to silence him.

Most of our doubts about our inadequacies don't come from the outside but from the deep recesses of our own minds. It is in our own minds that the gremlins lurk, holding us back from being the full, complete human beings we're meant to be, sending us messages and asking questions that make us feel weak and afraid.

Marva Collins, a remarkable, innovative teacher from the Chicago area, was inspired to teach children who were considered "unteachable." She realized that the first step for those children, who had experienced little success in their lives, was to overcome their self-doubt. In her "first-day-of-school" speech that she gave at the beginning of each school year, Marva Collins told her students, "The first thing we're going to do, children, is an awful lot of believing in ourselves."

So, how do you learn to believe in yourself? How do you respond to the interrogation of the Self-Doubt Gremlin? How do you take charge and silence the negative voices in your head?

You begin by making a list of your positive qualities. Think about yourself for a minute. Are you honest, thoughtful, a person of integrity? Are you caring, dependable, organized, friendly? Are you good at delegating, managing, planning? Are you responsible, enthusiastic, perceptive? Do you have a good sense of humor, a good sense of judgment, good taste? Are you trustworthy, fair, easygoing? Are you diligent, focused, creative, persistent? Are you intelligent, capable, fun? All of us have lots of positive qualities, and making a list forces us to acknowledge those qualities and claim them as our own.

Do you have any negative qualities? Of course, you do! But for now, just focus on the positive ones. It's the first step to believing in yourself.

Next, make a list of all the things you've accomplished in your life – everything from scoring the winning goal for your 4th grade soccer team to raising responsible kids. Everything from being a vice president of a large corporation to being president of the PTA. What leadership roles have you held? What jobs have you had? What awards have you received? What skills do you have? What honors have you been given? What are you good at doing? What have you done that gives you a sense of pride? This could take awhile! Listing everything you've done may take more time than you care to spend, but you get the point, don't you? Just as we all have positive qualities, we've all accomplished things – large and small, significant and trivial – that are to our credit. Make a list of what you've done, and that list will give you confidence for what you might do.

The next thing to consider is this: "If I try something, and I fail, what's the worst possible thing that could happen?" When you ask this question, you'll usually discover that the "worst possible thing" isn't really so bad. And besides, the things we fear usually don't happen.

OK, so what if there are some outside voices that sound a lot like the gremlins? Are there people in your life who are questioning you and your abilities? If so, how do you deal with them?

Make a list of those people, what they're saying, and why you think they might be discouraging you? Are they jealous? Threatened?

Afraid? Over-protective? Perhaps they have a genuine concern that you need to examine. When you get it down on paper and really analyze what's going on, you can usually identify the motive behind a person's lack of support, and once identified, it's easier to understand and deal with it.

Or maybe they're just plain wrong. I love the comments written in the notes of a movie studio executive after viewing the screen test of Fred Astaire. The movie executive wrote, "Can't act. Can't sing. Balding. Can dance a little." That should be a lesson to all of us. Even those people who are in positions of authority don't always know everything and can underestimate a person's abilities.

Yes, there are those who will attempt to discourage you, but based on personal experience, I'm convinced that we are our worst enemy. We sabotage ourselves by listening to the Self-Doubt Gremlin instead of the voice of reason and belief.

And finally, act as if you believe in yourself – even if you don't just yet. (When you read Chapter 4, you'll understand the powerful principle of "Acting As If.")

Believe in yourself. You're more talented, more capable, more intelligent, and more courageous than you think you are. Believe in yourself. Don't let your self-doubts keep you from making life count.

Make Life Count!

4

Act As If.

"When I'm really, really scared, I make believe I'm really, really brave. Sometimes it works."
Michael, age 5

"Confidence comes not only from where you've been. It also comes from where you expect to go."
Unknown

"We are what we pretend to be."
Kurt Vonnegut, Jr.

"Fake it 'til you make it."
Unknown

I read something recently that posed this question: "How would you act today if you were the most successful person in your community?" It went on to ask, "How would you dress? How would you walk? How would you use your time?" It's an interesting thought, isn't it? If you chose to, you could immediately become – by your actions – the kind of person you'd like to be.

Twenty-three hundred years ago, the Greek philosopher Aristotle proposed that actions precede reality. In other words, if you want to be brave, you "act as if" you're brave, and, sure enough, you are! If you want to be confident, "act as if" you're confident, and you are!

Anne was painfully shy. For her, the thought of going to a meeting or a social event and being surrounded by strangers was terrifying. But she realized that her shyness was keeping her from making friends and advancing her career. She was lonely and miserable. She was in a rut, and she wanted out.

Anne heard about the "act as if" principle and decided to give it a try. Even though she knew it wouldn't be easy, she was determined to do something. She was tired of being shy and desperately longed to be outgoing.

Her first step was to ask herself this question: "How does an outgoing person act?" Then, she wrote out the answer on a piece of paper. She concluded that an outgoing person walks briskly and confidently. An outgoing person holds her head up and seems anxious to make contact with others. An outgoing person smiles, greets everyone, and isn't hesitant to speak and introduce herself. An outgoing person asks questions, listens attentively, and focuses on the other person rather than herself.

Armed with this mental picture of how an outgoing person looks and acts, Anne was ready to give the "act as if" principle a try, and the opportunity soon presented itself. Anne's neighbors invited her to a cookout. In the past, she would have made up an excuse for why she couldn't attend, or she would have dropped by for just a few minutes, saying that she had to go to another function. This time, however, Anne decided to go to the party and pretend – "act as if" – she were outgoing, not the shy, withdrawn person that she was.

The results were amazing. By "acting as if" she were an outgoing person, she became one. Anne's actions created a new reality. And it wasn't nearly as difficult as she'd thought it would be. In fact, it was fun!

If you want to be outgoing, brave, confident, or successful, "act as if" you already are. Act your way into becoming what you want to be. Actions do, indeed, equal reality.

Make Life Count!

5

Do a Little Extra.

*"He who sows sparingly will reap sparingly,
and he who sows bountifully
will also reap bountifully."*
2 Corinthians 9:6

"Always do more than is required of you."
General George S. Patton

*"Some fragrance remains on the hand
that gives the rose."*
Chinese proverb

One of my favorite people is Eddy Victor. Eddy owns the dry cleaning shop where I've been taking my clothes for the last five or six years. Before I discovered Eddy, I'd been disappointed and dissatisfied with a number of other dry cleaners. The clothes weren't ready when they were promised; some were lost or damaged; buttons were often missing, and the proprietors never seemed to really care whether I was satisfied or not.

Then I met Eddy. Eddy is friendly and caring. His shop does good work. If I'm not totally satisfied with something, Eddy makes it right. He carries the clothes out to the car for me and does everything he can to make the experience of doing business with him pleasant.

Eddy also does a little extra. Recently, I took an American flag, circa 1917, to Eddy's shop. The flag was a 48-star one that had accompanied the casket of a World War I soldier home from Europe. The soldier was the son of a great aunt, and the flag was important to me. It had never been cleaned, and the aged fabric was fragile. It was very worn and frayed in spots, and I wanted to make sure that it got special treatment.

I didn't have to worry. When I picked it up, Eddy proudly showed me how he not only had cleaned the flag but also had carefully rolled it on a thick rod, tied it gently with string, and wrapped it in plastic to protect it. "So, Eddy," I said, "how much do I owe you?" I was prepared for a hefty bill, since I knew that giving the flag such special attention must have been painstaking work.

"You don't owe me anything," Eddy replied. "Wait a minute, Eddy," I said, "that's not right. Let me pay you something."

"No," he said, "I don't charge for American flags, not for my regular customers. I don't charge for Santa Claus suits," he chuckled. "I figure the person wearing that suit is doing something special for kids. I don't advertise this, but I also don't charge for clothes for a funeral. And," he said, "if I know that one of my young customers is going out for a job interview, I don't charge to clean his or her suit. It's my little 'good luck' gift to them."

As Eddy was telling me this, his smile and the twinkle in his eyes expressed the obvious joy he gets from giving "a little extra." I have a feeling that when Eddy provides "a little extra" for his customers, he has a great day.

Did you ever think that doing "a little extra," giving a little more than is required, may bring you greater pleasure than it brings the recipient? Try it, and see. It's just another way of having a great day and making life count.

6

Be Prepared.

"The greatest antidote to worry, whether you're getting ready for space flight or facing a problem of daily life, is preparation. The more you try to envision what might happen and what your best response and options are, the more you are able to calm your fears about the future."
John Glenn

"The future that we study and plan for begins today."
Chester O. Fischer

"There's no excuse for lack of preparation."
Lou Holtz

"You have to be ready to jump when the rope swings under your feet."
Unknown

Texas oilman Clint Murchison, Sr. was known for being a fast driver. Nothing slowed him down when he was in a hurry. One day Murchison was on the highway between Dallas and Athens, Texas, when he was pulled over by a highway patrol officer. As the officer was writing up the ticket, Murchison said, "Well, while you've got me here, you better write out another one, because I'm going to be coming back down this road a little while later."

Murchison believed in being prepared. He knew that he wasn't going to stop speeding, so he was just getting prepared for the consequences!

Are you prepared? The Boy Scout motto has great advice for all of us. People who have great days are prepared. They look ahead to the future and prepare for it. They equip themselves with the skills and the knowledge that they need.

Before a game, winning athletes prepare. Before an important meeting, a successful businessperson prepares. Before a party, a good hostess prepares. Before a speech, a good speaker prepares. Preparation means thinking about the future and how to deal with the opportunities and challenges ahead.

Paul "Bear" Bryant, the legendary coach of the University of Alabama, said, "Success is not a result of the will to win. Everyone has that. Great success comes as the result of the willingness to prepare to win." How true! The discipline of preparation is a key success factor.

Being prepared doesn't guarantee success, but lack of preparation is certainly a precursor to failure.

7

Enjoy the Moment.

*"All you have to do
is control the present moment.
It's all that matters."*
Unknown

"No pleasure ever lasts long enough."
Propertius

*"It is not how much we have
but how much we enjoy."*
Charles H. Spurgeon

*"The essence of happiness is pausing
to savor the gift of our present moments."*
David G. Myers, Ph.D.

"Life is short. Live it up!"
Nikita Khrushehev

New York City at Thanksgiving – what an extraordinary place to be! The city is decorated for the Christmas holidays, and thousands of people crowd the streets to watch the Macy's parade and to begin their holiday shopping.

Late in the afternoon on a Friday after Thanksgiving, my husband and I were among the throngs of people who were shoulder to shoulder shuffling down Fifth Avenue. We, like all the others who had waited for hours to get into museums and who had stood in long lines to make purchases at department stores, were growing weary and were beginning to lose our enthusiasm.

As the crowds were pushing us along, we found ourselves walking next to a man who was carrying a little girl on his shoulders. The little girl was probably four or five years old, and she was taking in all the hustle and bustle from her perch above the masses. As they walked next to us, I heard her ask her father, "Daddy, is this New York City?"

"Yes, honey, it is," he replied.

"Daddy," she exclaimed, "I'm having a blast!"

When I heard her expression of joyous enthusiasm for the moment, I thought, "I'm having a blast, too!" Yes, I was tired; yes, my feet hurt, and yes, I was weary of being jostled by this mass of humanity, but I, too, was having a blast. I had just lost sight of it, and that little girl's comment brought me back to reality.

Are you enjoying the moment? When you're at a restaurant, do you really savor the taste of the food – or do you just eat without any real attention to the joy of it? When you're on a trip, do you really notice the beauty or the uniqueness of your surroundings – or do you focus on the inconveniences that often go along with travel?

When you're at work, do you pay attention to the value of your contribution – or do you see only the frustrations of office politics and policies? When you're with your family, do you appreciate the moments with them – or do you take their presence for granted, thinking that they'll always be there?

Enjoy the moment! Have a blast! Focus on the moments – large and small – because, in truth, our lives are simply a collection of moments. We can choose to enjoy them or to let them pass unnoticed. Choose to enjoy the moment, and make life count.

Make Life Count!

8

Hang Out with Positive People.

"Keep no bad company."
Unknown

"A man is known by the company he avoids."
Unknown

*"Those who abandon their dreams
will discourage yours."*
Unknown

"I have an attitude, and I know how to use it."
Bumper sticker

"I don't suffer from stress, but I'm a carrier."
Unknown

*"Do not scorn the person who is
perpetually happy.
He does know something you don't."*
Paul Jones

D on't you love to be around people who are positive? You know who they are. They're the ones who are upbeat, enthusiastic, and fun. They're encouraging, energetic, and they look for the good in all situations.

But you know the others, too, don't you? We all know negative people who are discouraging, gloomy, and depressing. They never have a kind word to say. They're critical, pessimistic, picky, and they take a dim view of everything. They seem to feel that they're victims, the losers in life, and they let everyone know it. Being with them leaves us feeling drained.

In order to have great days, we need to "hang out with positive people." Of course, circumstances often force us to be with the ones who get us down, but when you have a choice – and you have more choices than you might think – choose to be with those who lift you up and encourage you.

When you absolutely have to be with the negative folks, when you can't possibly avoid the situation, refuse to be drawn into their world. Refuse to criticize, gripe, whine, or complain. Refuse to be brought down to their level. Counter their negative talk with positive talk.

Seek out those people who – like you – want to have great days. Because it is the people who want them that will have them.

9

Decide.

"Not to decide is to decide."
Harvey Cox

*"Though right or wrong, you're bound to find
Relief in making up your mind."*
Thornton Burgess

*"A wish changes nothing.
A decision changes everything."*
Unknown

"I've decided to come to work happy."
A wise person

D
o you have a hard time making decisions? I do. Our world is full of choices. For example, go to any grocery store, and unless you have a clear picture of what you want and which brand you prefer, you can be overwhelmed. Take salad dressing, for example. There are at least a dozen brands, each with 8-10 flavors, and each of those are available in regular, low fat, or no fat. Then, of course, you might want to factor in price and whether or not you have a coupon. Does the size of the bottle meet

your needs? Is the flavor one that most of the people in your family will like? As you can see, there are entirely too many decisions to make when it comes to determining what to put on your lettuce. Oh, yes, when you get to the checkout, you have to make another decision – paper or plastic!

In the scheme of things, deciding on a salad dressing is certainly easier than making the bigger decisions that we're required to make. For some people decision-making seems relatively easy; for others it's an agonizing experience.

The experts say that decision-making is a three-part process. You must first understand the objective, then look at the choices or alternatives, and finally consider the risk factors. Next time you're faced with a decision, try this method. At the top of a sheet of paper, write down the objective. What is it that you have to decide? What are your options? Draw a line down the center of the page; list the pluses for each option on one side and the minuses on the other. Next, determine how important the pluses and minuses are, including the risks involved. It's also helpful to set a deadline. Decide to decide by a certain date.

Do you know someone who's quit smoking or lost a lot of weight? Do you know someone who's established a successful exercise program or started a savings plan? When questioned, these people will usually say, "I just *decided* that I didn't want to be a smoker." "I just *decided* that I wanted to be thinner." "I just *decided* that I wanted to be more fit." "I just *decided* to save some money for my future." The act of deciding is always the first step toward accomplishing any goal or objective.

Is there something about which you need to make a decision? Not deciding can be frustrating and depressing. It can keep you from moving forward. So "just decide" that you're going to decide! Work through the process, and *decide* that you are going to live with your decision until it's time to make another one. There is "relief in making up your mind."

10

Realize That You Can Make a Difference.

"Make your life a mission...not an intermission."
Albert Glasgow

*"It's easy to make a buck.
It's a lot tougher to make a difference."*
Tom Brokaw

Every one of us has an opportunity every day to make a difference to the people with whom we come in contact. Whether we realize it or not, we are all making a difference – either positive or negative – all the time. Whether we realize it or not, people are being influenced by our words, our actions, and our attitudes.

You don't have to be famous. You don't have to be featured on the cover of a magazine. You don't have to have a fancy title or a corner office to be a positive influence in your own corner of the world.

Her name was Jean Fowler, but everyone at the law school at Emory University in Atlanta knew her as "Miss Jean." When I say everyone, I mean everyone – the first year students, the second years, the third years, the faculty, the staff – everyone knew Miss Jean, because she ran the snack shop in the law school. Students, staff, and faculty alike would stop by to get coffee, fruit, and sandwiches, and Miss Jean would provide nourishment not only for their bodies but also for their spirits.

I first learned about Miss Jean when our oldest son, Adam, was a student at Emory. Adam loved Miss Jean, but everyone loved Jean, because she always had a smiling face, a cheerful attitude, and an encouraging word. Jean had started working for Emory food services when she was eighteen, and at the time that Adam met her, she was in her sixties.

If you've ever spent much time around law students, you know that they can be a cantankerous bunch. They can be cynical, argumentative, combative, difficult, and generally, not too pleasant. In some respects, perhaps they're preparing for the challenges of their profession, but they're also in a very competitive environment. The final exam periods are particularly formidable; there's a lot at stake, and the stress level is high.

It was during final exams that Miss Jean seemed especially sensitive to the needs of her students. She knew that these jaded, defensive scholars needed some love, affection, and compassion; and no doubt, she was familiar with the adage that sometimes those who need love the most deserve it the least. When stressed-out, bleary-eyed students would come to her snack shop, Jean would caress them with her loving, warm, brown eyes, and in her soft, Southern drawl she'd say, "How you doin', baby? You look tired. Are you gettin' enough sleep? Now, baby, don't you worry 'bout those exams, because Miss Jean's gonna be prayin' for you," and her students knew that she would be.

Ironically, it was on Sunday morning during fall finals of Adam's last year at Emory that Miss Jean suffered a stroke while sitting in church. The news of her death spread like wildfire across the campus, and by afternoon, telephone messages and e-mails had traveled across the state of Georgia, the United States, and literally around the world to spread the news to former students that Miss Jean was gone.

In addition to the funeral service that was held at her church, a memorial service was held for Miss Jean at the law school at Emory. As you might expect, the first years, second years, third years, faculty, and staff attended the service. But also in attendance were powerful, successful attorneys and judges who came back to their alma mater to pay tribute to the woman who ran the snack shop, a woman who had made a positive difference in their lives.

Miss Jean was not an educated woman. She wasn't a celebrity or a high-profile individual. Her picture was never on the cover of a magazine; she didn't have a fancy title or a corner office, but none the less, Miss Jean was an influential person who made a positive difference in the lives of people in her corner of the world.

If you should ever have the opportunity to visit the law school at Emory, be sure to stop by the snack shop for a sandwich or a cup of coffee. It's now called "Jean's Place," and perhaps you'll be able to feel the positive spirit of a person who created great days every single day and who made her life count.

11

Choose Your Words Carefully.

*"Better to stumble with the toe
than with the tongue."*
Swahili proverb

*"Do not let any unwholesome talk come out
of your mouths, but only what is helpful
for building others up according to their needs,
that it may benefit those who listen."*
Ephesians 5:29

*"If you can't be kind, at least
have the decency to be vague."*
Unknown

*"Once a word has been allowed to escape,
it cannot be recalled."*
Horace

*"Set a guard over my mouth, O Lord;
keep watch over the door of my lips."*
Psalm 141:3

*"Resolve to stop shooting from the lip.
Words that you have to eat
can be hard to digest."*
Ann Landers

There is nothing more powerful than words. They are the source of great pleasure as well as great pain. They can start wars and prevent them. They can encourage or discourage. They can build up or break down. They can motivate or deteriorate. They can inspire and crush. Words are like fire; they can warm people or burn them.

The old adage, "Sticks and stones may break my bones, but words will never hurt me," isn't true. Words can hurt. They can also heal. What you say can change lives in either a positive or a negative way.

Choose your words carefully. Once they're said, they can't be retracted, and they will be remembered.

12

Be an Encourager.

*"He showed me what was possible,
and encouraged me to do it myself."*
Unknown

*"An anxious heart weighs a man down,
but a kind word cheers him up."*
Proverbs 12:25

Every day you have the opportunity to be an encourager. To "encourage" means "to give courage, hope, or confidence; to hearten," and you have the power to do that. You can be a positive influence. You can help people see positive traits in themselves that they don't see; you can let them know that you believe in them even when they don't believe in themselves.

Have you ever been encouraged by the words of another person? If so, honor that person today by being an encourager to someone else. Say to someone, "I believe in you" or "You can do it". It costs nothing, but the results are often priceless.

Be an encourager, and have a great day.

Make Life Count!

13

Pay Attention.

"Wake up and smell the coffee."
Unknown

When I leave home to go out of town for a speaking engagement, my husband always says three things. He always says, "Be careful; remember I love you; and pay attention to what's going on around you." His parting words remind me that he not only cares about me but also wants me to be safe.

But the concept of "paying attention to what's going on around you" can help you have great days. If you're paying attention, you'll notice the little things – new blooms in your flowerbeds, the smell of fresh brewed coffee, a cardinal in your backyard, the laughter of children at play, the smell of freshly mowed grass. If you're paying attention, you'll notice that someone needs a kind word or that a child or an elderly person needs some extra notice or care. If you're paying attention, you'll listen more carefully to catch the name of someone you're meeting for the first time; you'll be more attentive to the needs of your customers; you'll be more sensitive to the feelings of others, and you'll be more tuned in to life. If you're paying attention, you'll enjoy the music, the sunshine, and even the rain.

Pay attention to what's going on around you, and have a great day.

GREAT DAYS

14

Pray for Angels.

"A guardian angel o'er his life presiding,
Doubling his pleasures, and his cares dividing."
Samuel Rogers

"A good scare is worth more
to a man than good advice."
Edgar Watson Howe

I should probably confess to you *why* my husband always says, "Pay attention to what's going on around you." He tells me that each time I leave home, because he knows me very well. He knows that I have a tendency to get distracted. When I have a lot on my mind, I forget where I've parked the car. I lose track of the time. I misplace my luggage, my keys, my airline ticket – anything that's not attached. It's no wonder that my favorite bumper sticker reads, "Of all the things I've lost, I miss my mind the most!" That certainly could be my personal slogan.

While being distracted can be annoying, it can also be very scary. And it's at times like these that one needs an angel to come to the rescue.

A couple of years ago I was scheduled to do a program for one of my favorite clients in Columbia, Missouri. I flew to St. Louis, rented a car, and started driving west on Interstate Highway 70. It was early evening, and although I was a little bit hungry, I decided not to stop for dinner until I got to Columbia, which was about 130 miles away. However, I did stop to go to the restroom at one of the many McDonalds along the highway.

I arrived in Columbia about 8:45 p.m. and decided to get a take-out meal before I checked into my hotel. But when I stopped at the restaurant to get the food, I made a heart-stopping discovery. I didn't have my wallet.

Most of us have had one of those moments of sheer panic, one of those moments when it feels as if a giant hand has grabbed your insides and is squeezing the breath out of you, one of those moments when your heart is racing, and your head is spinning. Here I was alone, at night, in a strange city with no wallet – no money, no credit cards, no drivers license.

Since my client had made the hotel reservation, checking into the hotel wasn't a problem, but losing my wallet was! By this time, I had figured out that I must have left it in the restroom at McDonalds, but the question was – <u>which</u> McDonalds? I was in unfamiliar territory. I didn't even know the name of the exit where I'd stopped. I hadn't been paying attention to what was going on around me.

To make a long story short, with the help of the telephone information service and by making what seemed like dozens of calls to McDonalds all along the highway, I finally called one that was located in Warrenton, Missouri. I'm sure my voice revealed my state of panic to the manager who answered the phone. "By any chance," I asked, "did someone find a wallet? It might have been left in the ladies' room." I held my breath. It was getting late, and I was running out of options.

"What's your name?" the manager asked.

"Julie Alexander," I blurted out. "The wallet's black, and it has a Texas driver's license in it."

"Yes," said the manager. "It's right here. One of our senior citizen employees named Mary found it and turned it in."

The McDonalds was scheduled to close at 11:00 p.m., so I jumped in the car and sped toward Warrenton, hoping that I wouldn't be stopped by the highway patrol. When I arrived, minutes before closing time, the wallet was there with everything intact.

What a sense of joy, relief, and gratitude! What a feeling of thankfulness that, even when I wasn't "paying attention," I had an angel named Mary watching over me.

After the speaking engagement, on my way back to the St. Louis airport, I stopped at McDonalds, hoping to meet Mary. She was off that day, but I got her address and sent her a "thank you" note along with a monetary reward and a copy of my book, small payment for the kindness she showed me.

Perhaps one of the greatest blessings that came out of this scary incident was that Mary and I are now friends. We've corresponded several times, exchanged Christmas cards, and Mary has shared with me some poetry that she wrote. She even sent me a pair of embroidered pillowcases.

Thank God for honest people. Thank God for people like Mary. The moral of this story is, as my husband says, "Pay attention to what's going on around you," but if sometime you don't, pray for angels to be close at hand. And *be* an angel for others who need your help.

15

Eat Chocolate!

Q. "Why is there no such organization as
Chocoholics Anonymous?"
A."Because no one wants to quit."
Unknown

"Why bother with any other kind of cookie
when you can have a chocolate chip cookie?"
Jerry Fawcett

News Flash!

A recent study conducted by Harvard University School of Public Health concluded that eating chocolate may benefit one's health! The study, published in the British Medical Journal, focused on 7,841 Harvard male graduates and found that chocolate eaters live almost a year longer than those who abstain.

The researchers stress that their findings are preliminary. But I believe that there's enough conclusive evidence in that report to give the green light to those of us who believe that chocolate is one of the major food groups and to verify that it's a necessity for having a great day!

16

Establish Traditions.

"If we don't have Grandnonnie's sweet potatoes, I'm not eating Thanksgiving dinner."
Ben Alexander

"Because that's what we <u>always</u> do..."

What are the traditions that you have in your life? What are the special things that you do with your family or friends that mark holidays or special occasions? I have friends who always go to a movie on Christmas afternoon and others who always have lasagna for Christmas dinner. While those activities might seem untraditional to some folks, they're traditions that these families hold dear, and they're special and memorable for them.

I know one couple who celebrates their anniversary in the same way each year and others who host an annual Fourth of July gathering, complete with an elaborate fireworks show. Celebrating special occasions with special people in special ways makes

71

life...special. Certain activities and certain foods are a vital part of traditions, and traditions give comfort and stability to our lives. Traditions are important for children, for the elderly, for all of us. They are something to look forward to, something we can count on, and something that evokes memories of special times and special people.

On May 19, 1999, I received the following e-mail from my friend Kathleen. I think you'll enjoy her story about how she and her two friends, Beth and Marvelyn, continued a tradition. Kathleen wrote:

"Where were you at midnight? Well, let me tell you where I was. Beth, Marvelyn, and I were seated in a theater with our 25-year old sons – J.D., Christopher, and Derek. We were there for the opening of the new Star Wars movie, 'The Phantom Menace.' Why? Let me tell you...

Beth, Marvelyn, and I became friends when our boys started kindergarten twenty years ago. During that kindergarten year, the second Star Wars movie, 'The Empire Strikes Back' made its debut. Marvelyn always wants to see a movie the day it comes out. In fact, she wants to be there for the first showing on the first day. So, she, Beth and I decided that, since our boys were so excited about the movie, we would stand in line for tickets and take them out of school.

Then, they could be among the first to see 'The Empire Strikes Back.'

During the boys' fourth grade year, 'The Return of the Jedi' made its debut, and of course, Marvelyn stood in line to get tickets for the first show on the first day, and once again, we took the boys out of school for what had now become a tradition. Nothing of value comes easily, though. Marvelyn almost went to jail when someone questioned our right to hold places in line and to buy tickets in bulk, but we stood firm, and once again our boys were there...first show, first day.

As the hype began for 'The Phantom Menace,' we wondered if our boys would be able to get together again or if they would even want to. One was in law school; one was in college, and one was working...all in different cities. It probably wasn't going to happen. We moms thought, 'Oh, well, things change.'"

But as the opening day drew near, things did change. The one in law school graduated and happened to be in Dallas for a seminar the week the movie was opening. The one in college graduated and had accepted a job in Dallas. The one that was already working was working in Dallas. They were all in the same city at the same time, but they all had jobs, commitments, responsibilities, seminars. They probably couldn't take off just to see a movie.

But then we discovered that the first showing was going to be at one minute after midnight. That made it doable! The tradition continued.

Marvelyn was first in line to get tickets, and we were the first ones in our seats for the midnight show. So from midnight until 2:15 a.m., history was made. Maybe not history that will be in anyone else's history books but certainly in the hearts of three moms. And maybe somewhere in the hearts of these three young men, personal history was made. Maybe these young men learned what their mothers already know – that friends are a special part of your life, and they make your experiences more special.

As we moms held the places in line outside the theater, and as our sons played football in the parking lot waiting for the show to begin, we felt as if we had truly accomplished something. It wasn't about seeing the first show on the first day. It was about preserving a tradition among mothers and sons."

What traditions are you establishing for your family and friends? Are you making some memories? It's a sure way to have great days.

17

Lighten Up!

*"He overestimates his importance
in the scheme of things."*
Ken Alexander

*"When you get to heaven will you say,
'Why was I so serious back there?'"*
Dr. Bernie Segal

*"There are one hundred thousand million suns
in our galaxy and over a hundred thousand
million galaxies in the observable universe.
So I don't think that anything any one of us
may do is of overbearing importance."*
John Reid

Some people take the little challenges of life entirely too seriously, and they cause little things to become big things.

I know people – and I'll bet you do, too – who get unnecessarily upset over trivial matters. They seem to wear magnifying glasses; to them, everything appears to be a big deal. A broken fingernail, a lost sock, a run in a pair of pantyhose, a red light, an innocent comment from an acquaintance, an unintentional oversight – for some people these frivolous matters can be major issues. I've even seen some situations in which friendships have ended as the result of a dispute involving the color of the napkins to be used at a party!

For goodness sake, lighten up! With all the real problems, issues, and challenges in the world, let some of the little things go. We've all got enough to worry about without getting caught up in the insignificant. You've heard it said that a hundred years from now it won't make any difference, and the truth is that it probably doesn't make any difference now.

Focus on what's important...and have a great day!

18
Simplify.

*"What the world needs is more love
and less paperwork."*
Pearl Bailey

*"Have nothing in your house that you do not
know to be useful or believe to be beautiful."*
William Morris

*"I'd like to be a queen with a crown on my
head,but where would I put it
when I went to bed?"*
Pearl Wallace Chappell

*"A clean desk is a sign of a
cluttered desk drawer."*
Unknown

*"Home is where you keep your stuff
while you go out and buy other stuff."*
George Carlin

In its newsletter, the National Headache Foundation provides its readers with tips for reducing stress. One of those tips is, "Simplify, simplify, simplify." Good advice, but it's advice that's not easy for most of us to follow.

We live in a cluttered world. Our physical world is cluttered with stuff. Magazines that we haven't read yet – and probably won't read – as well as newspapers, clippings, junk mail, coupons, brochures, bank statements, and bills contribute to our disorganization.

Our closets are full of clothes we haven't worn in years and probably won't ever wear again. We save old T-shirts, sweaters, shoes, and handbags. Dresses that were bought during the Reagan administration and suits that have been too tight for too long are stashed and smashed in the closets along with memorabilia, this, that, and the other.

Our garages for full of tools and sports equipment that we haven't used – and probably won't – as well as gadgets and do-dads and thing-a-ma-gigs. A car in the garage? You've got to be kidding!

Those exercise bikes, weight benches, trampolines, and treadmills that we purchased with such enthusiasm and commitment now serve as clothes racks.

Our kitchen cabinets are packed with trendy appliances that seemed so necessary at the time of purchase. Now they simply take up space, get in the way, and become another source of frustration.

Let's face it – our lives are cluttered with things that, at one time, we didn't think we could live without, and now we're stressed out by having to live with them.

Our time is cluttered, too. Jobs, meetings, errands, events, activities, social engagements, obligations, commitments. We've said "yes" when we should have said "no," and now we have too much to do and not enough time to do it.

Does this sound familiar? It certainly does to me. Just like you, I often find myself on overload and enslaved to my time commitments and my stuff. The truth is that we have created our own prisons, but more importantly, we are the keepers of the keys. We can release ourselves by making some positive choices.

Begin today to simplify your life.

Clean out a closet. Throw away, or better yet, give away the things that long ago lost their usefulness or purpose or appeal to you. It might be just what someone else needs.

Begin to say "no" to commitments that aren't necessary, meaningful, or enjoyable. The first word a little child learns to say is "no," but somewhere along the way, we forget to say it, and we take on more than we really want or need or can effectively do.

Now I must confess that I'm writing this chapter in an office that has piles of papers, articles, notes, letters, bills, and miscellaneous this and that on the desk. Navigating through the piles on the floor is as challenging as tiptoeing through a minefield. So, if you'll excuse me, I'm going to stop right here, practice what I preach, and "simplify" by cleaning off my desk. Why don't you do the same?

A simpler life makes for great days.

19

Get Good at Getting Along.

*"It's great to be great,
but it's even greater to be human."*
Will Rogers

"A man reaps what he sows."
Galatians 6:7

*"This is the single greatest cause of difficulties
and deterioration in relationships – the need to
make the other person wrong or to
make yourself right."*
Dr. Wayne Dyer

"The worst prison would be a closed heart."
Pope John Paul II

*"We must learn to live together as brothers
or perish together as fools."*
Dr. Martin Luther King, Jr.

*"Do to others what you
would have them do to you."*
Matthew 7:12

G etting along is based on treating people with respect – respecting the thoughts, ideas, feelings, and opinions of those people closest to you, the people in your family and at work. It's based on communication, being able to address problems, challenges, differences of opinion in a calm, rational, and loving way. It's about listening intently with an open heart and mind. And it's about having values upon which you can agree.

In the best-selling book *Tuesdays with Morrie*, the elderly Morrie Schwartz gives us a reminder about relationships. He says, "If you don't respect the other person, you're gonna have a lot of trouble. If you don't know how to communicate, you're gonna have a lot of trouble. If you can't talk openly about what goes on between you, you're gonna have a lot of trouble. And if you don't have a common set of values in life, you're gonna have a lot of trouble." Morrie pretty well sums up the basic tenants of getting good at getting along.

In his book *The Pursuit of Happiness*, Dr. David G. Myers says that it is the people in our lives that bring us our greatest pleasure as well as our greatest pain. In a survey, people were asked what had caused them the most stress in the last week, to which the majority answered, "Family." They were also asked what had brought them the greatest joy. Their answer? You guessed it – "Family."

Research tells us that people who describe their work environment as supportive and cooperative are happier in their jobs. So, in both cases, our happiness and satisfaction have a lot to do with how well we get along.

How good are you at "getting along" with the people in your life? If you are demanding, have a closed mind, or are quick to anger, chances are you're not very good. If you're disrespectful, rude, and self-centered, chances are you're not having too many great days.

Get good at getting along by opening your eyes, your ears, your mind, and your heart to the people in your life, and I'll guarantee you'll have more great days.

Make Life Count!

Be Committed.

*"Few things are impossible to diligence.
Great works are performed not by strength,
but by perseverance."*
Samuel Johnson

"The greatest victory is victory over self."
Publius Syrus

*"They will soar on wings like eagles;
they will run and not grow weary,
they will walk and not be faint."*
Isaiah 40:31

I f you were to look up the definition of "commitment," you might find a picture of Walt Byerly. Walt is a living, breathing example of what it means to be committed.

About twenty-seven years ago, Walt was feeling out of shape. He knew he needed more exercise, so he decided to take up jogging. At first, it was a struggle. He had to work long and hard to be able to jog nonstop for one mile. As time passed, he increased his distance to two miles and began to see the benefits of his fitness program.

On November 5, 1974, Walt asked himself a question. "I wonder if I could jog two miles a day for 365 days without missing a single day?" He made a commitment to do it, and he did.

But Walt is a person who likes to challenge himself and to raise the bar to continually improve his performance. So, he decided to do it again the next year and the next and the next. On November 5, 1999, Walt Byerly celebrated an anniversary. On that day, he had jogged at least two miles a day *every* day for twenty-five consecutive years! And he's still going.

For eighteen and half of those years, Walt jogged *four* miles a day. He's logged a lot of miles, and he's kept detailed records. Nothing has prevented him from keeping his commitment. He's never allowed weather, illness, injuries, workload, or early morning airline flights to deter him. Walt has jogged all over the United States, in almost every country in Europe, in Communist countries, around campfires in the wilderness, and on the decks of cruise ships. In fact, you could say he's jogged around the world, because his mileage totals more than the circumference of the earth, which is 24,900 miles.

Like all of us, Walt's had his share of challenges, and he's used his jogging time to think, to plan, and to pray. But most of his prayers are for the needs of others. Every day he prays for the more than two hundred people that he has on the prayer list that he keeps in his head and in his heart. Walt says that praying for others has been one of the most exciting things he's ever done.

What has being committed done for Walt? Commitment to his prayer list has brought him not only closer to God but also closer to people on his list. Commitment to his fitness routine has given him amazing stamina, good health, and lots of energy. And his streak of consecutive days of jogging gives him a great sense of accomplishment. His good health allows him to work hard all day and function on six hours or six-and-a-half hours of sleep. He's optimistic and excited about life.

Walt's commitment carries over into his real estate business. His clients know that they can count on him to take care of their needs and to do what he says he'll do. He's committed to his wife, his three children, and his eight grandchildren. He's committed to his church and to community service.

To what are you committed? In what areas of your life are you disciplined and consistent? Starting today, be totally, unwaveringly committed in one or two areas, and like Walt Byerly, see how the habit of commitment can spill over into other facets of your life. Being committed to the important things makes life count.

Make Life Count!

21

Don't Criticize.

"He who slings mud loses ground."
Unknown

"If you find fault, lose it."
Julie Alexander

*"People ask you for criticism,
but they only want praise."*
William Somerset Maugham

*"Parents don't realize how they can nag
and pick at a child until there's
nothing left to pick."*
Marva Collins

*"Man invented language to satisfy
his deep need to complain."*
Lily Tomlin

*"If you haven't got something nice to say
about someone, come and sit next to me."*
Alice Roosevelt Longworth

How quick we are to criticize. How quick we are to seek out a weakness in someone and pounce on it, as we say in Texas, "like a duck on a June bug."

How quick we are to find fault rather than to look for what is good and right and positive in others.

Maybe we think that by tearing others down, we build ourselves up. Maybe those feelings of self-doubt that we discussed earlier create such insecurities that we try to make ourselves look good by making others look bad.

Whatever the reason, being critical of or finding fault in others achieves no positive purpose. The only thing it does is to degrade and devalue the one who's doing the criticizing.

Marva Collins, the teacher whom I mentioned earlier, made a point of finding something to praise in each one of her students every day. It wasn't always easy. Her students were difficult and had multiple problems as a result of their intellectual challenges as well as their home environments, but every day Marva Collins found something to praise. She encouraged them with praise rather than humiliating them with criticism.

As a parent, a spouse, a supervisor, a neighbor, a business owner, a teacher, an in-law, a community leader, an employee, a grandparent, a child – are you praising or criticizing the people in your life? When we praise rather than criticize, people tend to want to live up to that acclaim. Find something to praise in each person that you encounter today. You'll make it a great day for yourself and all the people you meet.

Dale Carnegie said, "Any fool can criticize, condemn, and complain – and most fools do."

Make Life Count!

22

Do Something!

"Do or don't do; there is no try."
Yoda

*"Our inaction often leaves us in the dark.
The light is there. All we have to do is
get up and flip the switch."*
Unknown

"Well done is better than well said."
Benjamin Franklin

*"A good plan violently executed right now is
far better than a perfect plan
executed next week."*
General George S. Patton

*"Action may not always bring happiness,
but there is no happiness without action."*
Benjamin Disraeli

"Never mistake motion for action."
Ernest Hemingway

People who have great days are action-oriented. They're decisive. They have a plan, and they act on that plan. At the end of the day, they can look back with pride on what they've accomplished, and doing so generates energy to keep the process going.

A law of physics says that an object in motion will tend to stay in motion, and we human beings abide by that same law. Have you ever noticed that getting started on a project is the hardest part? Once you get going, you can keep going. You get into the flow of the work and can keep working productively for an extended period of time.

Mihaly Csikszentmihalyi, a psychologist at the University of Chicago, coined the word "flow" to describe the state of being totally absorbed in one's work. In that state, one is often unaware of the passage of time or even noise or distractions in the environment. In this state a person does his or her best work, work that is creative and even fun.

But no one can achieve "flow" until he or she takes action. We have to do the "jump-start" first; we have to take action, get in gear, *do something.*

People who have great days are active people. They're involved in work, projects, hobbies, social events, community activities, sports, their church, volunteerism, continuing education classes. What are you doing? Do *something* – and have a great day! Make life count!

23
Do Nothing.

*"There is no pleasure in having nothing to do;
the fun is in having lots to do and not doing it."*
Mary Little

*"Perhaps the best way to thank God for the gift
of living is to appreciate the present hour, to sit
quietly and hear your own breathing and look
out on the universe and be content."*
Lin Yutang

Another way to have a great day is to do nothing. No plans, no projects, no pushing. Sit, think, breathe, observe, contemplate, meditate, reflect, pray.

Be grateful. Be peaceful. Be silent.

"Be still and know that I am God."
Psalm 46:10

GREAT DAYS

24

Don't Litter.

"Keep America Beautiful"

"Don't Mess with Texas"
Anti-littering campaign slogan

One of my pet peeves is people who litter. Paper cups, cans, sacks, debris along the roadways, in the parks, and on the streets is disgusting. Whenever I see someone throw trash out of his or her car window, I get furious!

Take this as a warning: Don't ever let me see you discarding trash in an inappropriate way. You'll be in more trouble than you can handle!

Keep the world clean and beautiful, and have a great day.

25

Dance.

*"It is a fine thing to find a man who loves you,
but a truly extraordinary thing to find
a man who will dance with you."*
Ann Patchett

"No sane man will dance."
Cicero

"If they play the Twist, I'll get up and dance."
Ken Alexander

"Do ya, do ya, do ya, do ya wanna dance?"
Bobby Freeman

Here's an idea for having a great day. Put on some music and dance!

When I was in college, I took a physical education course called "Modern Dance." I had wanted to take co-ed volleyball, but when it was my turn to register, the class was full, so I signed up for "Modern Dance" by default. The class was taught by a wiry, wisp of the woman named Kitty Wingo. Miss Wingo, who must have been at least seventy years old, was a campus institution. She had taught in the physical education department for years, and her dance classes were legendary.

Dressed in her black leotards and sometimes wearing a long scarf around her neck for a dramatic effect, she would fill the gymnasium with music and say, "Dance, girls! Dance! Pretend you are trees swaying in the breeze. Let the music carry you away."

Now, I have to admit that as a college freshman, I thought this whole concept was ridiculous, and my classmates and I had to struggle to control our snickering. We thought Miss Kitty Wingo had gone over the edge!

Miss Wingo was a bit eccentric, but I also have to admit that maybe she was on to something. She, certainly more than her 18-year-old students, knew the joy of dancing. She knew that a little "swaying to the music" was good for the soul.

When you're in the dumps, turn on the music and dance! You can dance in your kitchen, your living room, your bedroom, on your back porch – it really doesn't matter. You don't even need a partner. Choose any music you like – rock 'n roll, country, polka, flamenco, ballet, a waltz – whatever suits your mood.

Dancing will lift your spirits, maybe cause you to laugh a little, and you'll have a great day!

26

Laugh.

"Comedy is tragedy plus time."
Carol Burnett

"If we couldn't laugh, we'd all go insane."
Jimmy Buffett

*"The human race has one really effective
weapon,and that is laughter."*
Mark Twain

*"Among those whom I like or admire,
I can find no common denominator,
but among those whom I love, I can.
All of them make me laugh."*
W.H. Auden

*"There is a time for everything...
...a time to weep and a time to laugh."*
Ecclesiastes 3:1, 4

"Laughter is a tranquilizer with no side effects."
Unknown

*"Laugh...and the class laughs with you,
but you stay after school alone."*
Unknown

I'm convinced that there are a lot of funny things going on in your world! I know there are in mine. Every day and in every situation, particularly the difficult ones, I really try to look for humor, and I usually find it. Trying to seek out the humor helps me keep things in perspective and not get so stressed over the things I can't control.

One day I was doing an after-lunch speech for a large group. This is always a challenging time slot to be in, because no matter how interesting, entertaining, dynamic, and motivating the speech, the combination of the 1:00 o'clock time slot and a full stomach means "nap time" for many people.

On this particular occasion, a woman who was sitting at the center, front table went to sleep. Now, this wasn't just a "nod-your-head, drift-off" kind of sleep. This was a "throw-your-head-back," *snoring* kind of sleep. And her slumber didn't go unnoticed. Everyone around her was aware of what was going on, and they were embarrassed for her and for me. The people on either side of her took it upon themselves to attempt to rouse her. They took turns giving her a nudge, which only caused her to change position, snort loudly, and go right back to sleep.

I could have been angry, insulted, and infuriated by her behavior, but instead, I chose to view the situation with amusement. I chose to see the humor.

When the program was over and the applause began, she woke up. And she was one of the first people to come rushing up. "Oh, honey," she said, "I enjoyed your speech so much. You are so refreshing."

I smiled and thanked her for the compliment. But inside, I was laughing. It was obvious to me that what had left her feeling so "refreshed" was not my speech but her nap!

Are you looking for reasons to laugh? Do you choose to see the things that happen in your life with a sense of humor, or do you choose to take life...and yourself...too seriously? A high school principal gave a new teacher some very good advice. He said, "If you don't have a sense of humor, you'll be angry all the time."

Look for the humor...and have a great day!

27

Take a Nap.

"Listen...Do you hear it?
It's the 'call of the covers.'"
Ken Alexander

"Fatigue makes cowards of us all."
Vince Lombardi

One of life's great pleasures is a nap. Whether it's a short, energizing catnap or a long, rainy Sunday afternoon siesta, a little shut-eye is a very good thing. There are even some large corporations that are encouraging their employees to close their office doors, close their eyes, and take a short nap to revitalize their spirits and their creative energy.

Life's too short to spend it all awake! Take a nap...and have a great day!

28

Get Up and Get Going!

*"The easiest way to make ends meet
is to get off yours."*
Unknown

"Success doesn't come to you. You go to it."
Marva Collins

"The desire to do something doesn't get it done."
Unknown

"70% of life is showing up."
Woody Allen

*"There is no perfect time to start something.
Don't wait. The time will never be just right."*
Napoleon Hill

*"I believe that the difference between great
people and everyone else is that great people
create their lives actively, while everyone else
is created by their lives, passively waiting to
see where life takes them next."*
Michael E. Gerber

"Get busy living, or get busy dying."
The Shawshank Redemption

There are a lot of people in the world who seem to sit around waiting for something good to happen. They wait for their ship to come in; they wait for times to get better; they wait for relationships or their job circumstances to improve. They're stifled and consumed by laziness, inactivity, indecisiveness, and procrastination.

In order to have great days and to make life count, we have to take action. We've got to get up and get going. We've got to stop putting off getting on with life. One of my favorite bumper stickers reads, "Warning: Dates on calendars are closer than they appear." Isn't that the truth?

The Roman thinker, writer, and philosopher Seneca wrote, "While we are postponing, life speeds by." What a sobering thought. What are you waiting for? Get up and get going! Make life count!

29

Do What
You Love.

*"When you can connect talent with what you
love to do, you're in a state of grace."*
Bill Gove

*"When love and skill come together,
expect a masterpiece."*
John Ruskin

*"Basically, I no longer work for anything
but the sensation I have while working."*
Albert Giavometti, Sculptor

*"In order to succeed, you must know
what you are doing, like what you are doing,
and believe in what you are doing."*
Will Rogers

*"The crowning fortune of a man is to be born
to some pursuit which finds him employment
and happiness, whether it be to make baskets,
or broadswords, or canals, or statues, or songs."*
Ralph Waldo Emerson

W hen *Sports Illustrated* celebrated its
fortieth anniversary, the magazine
featured an article that focused on

forty athletes who had been highly successful in a variety of sports during this four-decade period of time. Each was asked, "What was it that made you so successful? What was it that drove you to be the best?" Although their answers were expressed in a variety of ways, the message was the same. Each of those athletes succeeded, because they <u>loved</u> what they did.

You may be saying, "Well, it's easy for athletes to love what they do. They're playing a game, and besides they're rich and famous and get special privileges. They're celebrities."

But I recently heard about a man who'd worked at the same job for thirty-three years. For thirty-three years, he'd worked in the same warehouse. As a young man, his job had been to stack boxes on the shelves, and in his later years, he drove a forklift. When he retired, it was noted that in his lengthy career, he had never missed a single day of work. When questioned about it, he said, "I always wanted to be there to do my job. I wanted to be there every day, because I love what I do." Apparently money and status have little to do with whether one loves their work.

One day I was presenting a seminar at a meeting for school administrators and principals. I asked each person to share with the group what had drawn them to education.

Why did they choose this challenging profession? The most dramatic story was told by one of the principals whom we'll call Joe.

When Joe was in the sixth grade, he adored the principal of his school. He thought this man was tops, and he wanted to be just like him when he grew up. He, too, wanted to work with students and teachers. He wanted to be an example, a leader, a role model who would shape the lives of young people just as his principal was shaping his.

As Joe was finishing high school and preparing to go to college, his parents and his friends began questioning his career choice. "Why would a sharp guy like you want to be a principal?" they said. "There's no money in it; there's a lot of stress. You can be a lot more successful doing something else." And Joe began to listen to these "voices of reason" instead of the voices in his own head and his own heart.

At college he majored in business, and after graduating, he took a job with a growing company. After more than ten years with the company, Joe was doing well. From a financial standpoint and by the world's definition, he was "successful." But Joe really wasn't happy; every day was a grind.

But all that changed one day while Joe was coming home from a business trip. His plane went down in a rice field. Fortunately, he walked away from the crash site. But that incident would be life changing. As he stumbled through the watery field, he promised himself that he would not spend another day doing what he hated.

Joe quit his job, went back to school, became certified in education, and today he's living out his dream. No, he's not making as much money as he once did; yes, there's a lot of stress, but for Joe, he's doing what he loves, and every day is a great one. He's making life count.

30

Get Over It.

"The heaviest load you'll ever carry is a grudge."
Julie Alexander

*"Nobody ever forgets where he
buried the hatchet."*
Kin Hubbard

"Happiness is good health and a bad memory."
Ingrid Bergman

*"Bear with each other and forgive whatever
grievances you may have against one another.
Forgive as the Lord forgave you."*
Colossians 3:13

Have you ever had someone hurt your feelings? Have you ever had someone cheat you or lie to you or steal from you? Have you ever had someone set you up for failure? Have you ever had someone break your heart? Have you ever had someone take advantage of you? Have you ever had things happen to you that you didn't expect or want? Of course, you have. All of us have been hurt, stabbed in the back, or "done wrong" by someone else or by the circumstances of life.

But until you "get over it," you can never really be happy or content.

In some of my programs, I introduce the audience to "the Grudge." The Grudge is a little purple creature with funny eyes and a topknot on its head. It looks very innocent, and when people first see it, they think it's cute. But there's more to the Grudge than meets the eye.

I'll sometimes invite a volunteer to come to the front and ask that person to hold the Grudge in one hand. The volunteer is always shocked to discover how heavy the Grudge is. It looks so small and so soft. One wouldn't think that it would be much of a burden, but in reality, it weighs about eight pounds. At first, the weight of the Grudge is bearable, but after awhile, it gets heavier and heavier, and holding it becomes a chore. Isn't that the way it is with grudges? The longer we hold on to them, the heavier they become and the more miserable we become.

Is there someone against whom you're holding a grudge? If so, get over it. No purpose is being served, and the only person being hurt by it is you. Let it go. Free yourself from the burden. As long as you carry around a grudge, as righteous and as justified as it may seem, you can't have great days.

31

Be Purposeful.

*"Happiness is loving what you do,
and knowing it matters."*
David G. Myers, Ph.D.

*"If you don't have a plan, you'll be
a stepping stone for those who do."*
Phil McGraw, Ph.D.

*"Man is only happy as he finds
a work worth doing and does it well."*
E. Merrill Root

*"Every person is born for a purpose.
Everyone has a God-given potential, in essence,
built into them. And if we are to live life to its
fullest, we must realize that potential."*
Norman Vincent Peale

D
o you know what your purpose is?
Do you know the answer to the
question, "Why am I here?"

That's a pretty heavy question, and being confronted with it makes most of us more
than a little uneasy. Most folks don't know
the answer because: a) They've never thought
about it, or b) Thinking about it makes them
feel inadequate or insignificant.

Most of us don't feel that we've been put on this earth to do great things. Or if we suspect that we are here to accomplish something important, we feel guilty because we feel that we haven't done it. Most of us think that if we aren't a great composer or a brilliant surgeon or a research scientist discovering a cure for cancer or a Mother Theresa caring for the poor, then we don't really have much of a purpose.

The truth is, though, that all of us are put here for a reason. We're not here just to take up space. Each of us is important in the scheme of things. As Dr. Peale suggests in the quote above, if we're going to live life to the fullest, if we're going to have great days, if we're going to make life count, we must know what that purpose is and then be *purposeful* in our living.

Let's look at being purposeful in your job. What's the purpose of your job? If you're a teacher, a doctor, a caregiver, a preacher, perhaps it's easy for you to realize that your vocation has a positive purpose. But in many jobs, it's not always that clear. You may have difficulty seeing what you consider to be any real importance in your job. But if you step back and think about it, you'll be able to find purposefulness in your vocation.

Several years ago I worked with the environmental services department of a large hospital. For the most part, the employees in this department had little education, fairly low salaries, and very low self-esteem. They didn't think they were important. They didn't see their jobs as purposeful, and their work and their attitudes reflected that point of view.

But their jobs were important. It was their responsibility to make sure that the hospital was a clean, safe, pleasant place. It was their job to create a sanitary, hazard-free environment for the patients and their families, as well as the hospital employees. In many respects, their jobs were some of the *most* important. When these people began to see their work from a fresh perspective, and when they began to realize that what they did every day made a positive difference, they felt better about themselves and took more pride in their work. They had more great days.

I recently talked with a woman who felt that her job had no real purpose or significance. She worked in the data processing department of a large insurance company. All day long she entered policyholder information in the company's database. To her, what she did all day was meaningless and irrelevant.

As we talked, I said "Sandra, have you ever stopped to think about the people whose information you're handling? Each one has had a problem – an auto accident, a fire, perhaps an illness or the death of a loved one. Each one has a challenge, or they wouldn't have filed a claim. Did you ever think about the fact that your entering their data quickly and accurately is a great service to them? They need to have their claims paid as quickly as possible, and if you're accurate in your work and do your job well, that's one less problem, one less hassle they have to face." Seeing the purposefulness of her job gave Sandra a fresh perspective and made her realize that her work was far more important than she had imagined.

What is your purpose? Perhaps you were placed on this earth to be a caring volunteer, to be a dedicated teacher, to be an advocate for fairness, to bring music or laughter to the world. Perhaps your purpose is to create beauty, to make your environment clean and safe, to build the self-esteem of others by helping them improve their appearance, to be a loving caregiver to children or the elderly. Perhaps you're here to create new technology, to help people secure their future through wise investments, to interpret and uphold the law, to raise responsible children, or like me, to help people learn how to have great days.

In his book *The On-Purpose Person*, Kevin McCarthy writes, "Purpose is energy. It's the single most motivating force there is. Discover your purpose, be on-purpose, and you will have a life filled with meaning and significance." What that really means is this: when you know your purpose and live purposefully, you'll have more great days. And you'll make life count!

32

Choose to be Cheerful.

*"A cheerful heart is good medicine,
but a crushed spirit dries up the bones."*
Proverbs 17:22

*"I can please only one person per day.
Today is not your day.
Tomorrow isn't looking good either."*
Message on a poster

*"Start every day with a smile,
and get it over with."*
W.C. Fields

*"If you come home dog tired at the end
of the day, maybe you've been
growling all day."*
Unknown

*"Take care that the face which looks out
from your mirror in the morning is a
pleasant face. You may not see it
again all day, but others will."*
Unknown

"Pain is inevitable; misery is a choice."
Unknown

> *"It is not what happens to you,*
> *but how you react to it that matters."*
> Epictetus

No matter what kind of a day you're having, you have a choice as to how you're going to respond to it. You can choose to be angry, miserable, or depressed. You can choose to gripe, whine, or complain. You can choose to sulk, criticize, or degrade. You can choose to belittle or bemoan. You can choose to feel sorry for yourself. You can choose to be a victim.

Or, you can choose to be cheerful. All of us have days when Murphy's Law grabs us by the throat, those days when everything that could possibly go wrong does. But the people who are successful survivors, the ones who have great days, are those who choose to be cheerful.

You've no doubt heard the term "mindset." I really like the idea that we can set our minds however we choose. It's as if we have an attitude meter in our heads, and we can set that meter to determine how we respond to the world around us. What's your mindset? Are you choosing to be cheerful and positive, or are you choosing to be gloomy and negative?

The choice is yours. Choose to be cheerful, and have a great day.

33

Push Yourself.

"No pressure, no diamonds."
Mary Case

*"There is no use whatsoever trying to help
people who do not help themselves.
You cannot push anyone up a ladder
unless he is willing to climb himself."*
Andrew Carnegie

"It's kinda fun to do the impossible."
Walt Disney

*"Attempt the impossible in order
to improve your work."*
Bette Davis

*"I can do everything through him
who gives me strength."*
Philippians 4:13

Are you too easy on yourself? Do you frequently give yourself a break, let yourself off the hook, or fail to hold yourself accountable? Most of us are far more lenient with ourselves than we would ever be with others.

In what areas of your life do you need to push yourself, to be a little tougher on yourself?

At work, are you doing your best, giving your best effort every single day? Perhaps the real question is, would you hire you?

Are you taking care of yourself physically? Are you exercising even when you don't feel like it? Are you eating what you should instead of what you want?

All things that are worthwhile take effort, sacrifice, maybe even a little pain, but the payoff is worth it. Michael Flatley, the creator of the musical productions *Lord of the Dance* and *Riverdance,* pushes his performers to be their best. Perfection is the only acceptable level of performance. The practices are long, grueling, and often painful experiences, but Flatley says, "If you start making excuses for the pain, you'll never accomplish anything."

DeLynn Parker is a young woman who had it all. She had a great husband, three precious sons, lots of friends, a beautiful home in an affluent neighborhood, a comfortable lifestyle. Her husband's successful career allowed her to be a stay-at-home mom and to participate in church and community activities. Her life was easy; in fact, she thought, maybe too easy. So DeLynn decided to push herself. She decided to run a marathon.

While she'd been a recreational runner for a number of years, she'd never considered long-distance running until several friends from college suggested the idea of running a marathon in Washington, DC. DeLynn was thirty-five at the time, and she was ready for a challenge.

As she began to train, DeLynn began to see parallels between the training and her life experiences. She saw how her running could impact her and her family in a significant way. For her, four phases of running the marathon – the fear of the unknown, the support of family and friends, the physical pain of the experience, and the reward and ultimate high of accomplishing the goal – seemed to symbolize her first pregnancy and the birth of her first child. So she decided to dedicate the marathon to her firstborn son who was nine at the time. She even took him to Washington to watch her compete in the race.

Of course, mothers are determined to be "fair" when it comes to their children. Since she had two other sons, it seemed only fitting that she should run two more marathons, one for each of her other boys. The second race came just two months after the first. For her, this event was intense, fast, very emotional – characteristics that seemed to match her second son's personality.

Her third son, who was three at the time, was going through a phase in which he wore cowboy boots all the time – with shorts, his swimsuit, even his "birthday" suit! How appropriate it was that his race was the Cowtown Marathon in Fort Worth, Texas, and the trophy was shaped like a cowboy boot!

By this time, DeLynn was hooked on running and decided to do one marathon for each son every year. But, in the meantime, she became pregnant again, and – you guessed it – another son, another marathon! Four every year!

How does she do it? DeLynn says she can do it because she trains smart; she knows what she has to do to prepare, and she does it. With a hint of laughter in her voice, she says, *"Sometimes people say 'How do you do it?' or 'I'm in awe of what you do.' But it's really just putting one foot in front of the other. No one should feel intimidated. It's something anyone can do. In fact,"* she says, *"I try to encourage others to run a marathon. If I can do it, they can, too."*

Maybe the real question is *why* does she do it? After running nine marathons in the past three and a half years, DeLynn has many reasons. First, she does it for her family. Her husband and her four sons are her encouragers; they push her to keep going, to keep trying. They're her cheerleaders.

She does it, too, to be a role model, to show her sons that accomplishing worthwhile goals takes time, hard work, and effort and that winning the victory doesn't come easy. As the only female in the family, she also wants to be an example to her sons of a strong, focused woman.

Her sons all play sports; her husband coaches their teams. As an athlete herself, she can meet them on their level and understand and be a part of their world.

But there's another thing that keeps DeLynn Parker running. Running marathons is her way of remembering that her strength comes from God and of being dependent on Him. She says, *"I've had some challenges in my life. My mother died of breast cancer at an early age, and there have been other difficult times. During those times, I had to depend on my faith to get me through. But in the last few years, life has been so good. Of course, there are the daily challenges of raising four young sons, but the blessings have certainly outweighed the challenges. By depleting all my physical and mental reserves, the running forces me to depend on God, because I know I can't do it alone."*

DeLynn says, *"The human body isn't designed to run nonstop for twenty-six miles, and the last six are the most grueling. Those last six miles are totally mental. It's your mind that gets you through. And it's at mile twenty that I begin to pray even more fervently than I do in the earlier part of the race. That's when I recite scriptures and sing songs. It's an out-of-body experience. God is my running partner, and I rely on Him to carry me to the finish line."* DeLynn is convinced that this strategy and attitude is what enabled her to qualify for and run in the Boston Marathon.

In what areas of your life do you need to push yourself? What are the benefits or the rewards that it would bring, not only to you but also to the people in your life?

To achieve the extraordinary things, to be successful in areas that some might see as impossible takes commitment and a "no excuses" attitude. It means pushing yourself to get where you want to go and not giving up when the going gets tough.

So, push yourself, and see where it takes you. Push yourself, and make life count!

34

Pamper Yourself.

*"Hard work never killed anyone...
but why take chances."*
Unknown

*"If at first you don't succeed,
destroy all evidence that you tried."*
Unknown

*"I decided long ago never to look at the
right hand side of the menu or the price tag of
clothes – otherwise I would starve, naked."*
Helen Hayes

*"A private railroad car is not an acquired taste.
One takes to it immediately."*
Eleanor R. Belmont

You certainly can't push yourself all the time, so occasionally, pamper yourself. Spend some time today doing something that you really like to do. Spoil yourself a little.

What are some little indulgences that you enjoy? Maybe it's a manicure, a pedicure, or a bubble bath. Maybe it's an ice cream cone, a chocolate truffle, a nap, or a movie. Maybe it's a round of golf in the middle of the week, dinner with friends, or an afternoon alone. Maybe it's spending time with a special friend, reading a new novel, or puttering in the garden. Maybe it's exploring a new store or visiting a museum. Maybe it's test-driving an expensive sports car or riding a horse. Maybe it's buying a new pair of shoes, taking your dog for a walk, purchasing some fluffy new towels, listening to your favorite music. Maybe it's painting or singing or hiking or just being.

Have you figured it out yet? Great days are the result of a balance of seriousness and fun, of doing something and doing nothing, of pushing and pampering. So for today, pamper yourself a little...and have a great day.

35

Eat More Chocolate!

*"Some say chocolate is their weak point;
I say chocolate is my strong point."*
Dolley Madison

"Never eat more than you can lift."
Miss Piggy

36

Don't Whine.

"Realize that if you have time to whine and complain about something, then you have time to do something about it."
Anthony J. D'Angelo

"I can't complain, but sometimes I still do."
Joe Walsh

"Do everything without complaining or arguing."
Philippians 2: 14

Whiners are annoying. They gripe and complain about everything. Nothing is right. They never see any good in anything and seem to find fault in everything. Whiners don't want to accept the responsibility for fixing the problem; they just want to complain about it.

If you're a whiner, stop it! Change what you can; accept the things you can't, and give the people around you a break. Whining solves nothing and creates a lot of misery.

Stop whining...and have a great day.

37

Be Enthusiastic.

*"A man can succeed at almost anything
for which he has unlimited enthusiasm."*
Charles Schwab

"I'm so excited!"
The Pointer Sisters

*"Nothing is so contagious as enthusiasm;
it moves stone, it charms brutes.
Enthusiasm is the genius of sincerity,
and truth accomplishes no victory without it."*
Edward George Earle Bulwer-Lytton

*"Nobody grows old merely by living
a number of years.
We grow old by deserting our ideals.
Years may wrinkle the skin,
but to give up enthusiasm withers the soul"*
Samuel Ullman

What are you excited about today? What inspires you? Do you have a real sense of enthusiasm for your life, your job, your relationships? Are you enthusiastic about a trip, a project, an upcoming event? Do you have an intense interest in politics, a cause, a hobby, a sport?

People who have great days are those who are enthusiastic about something. Whether it's a cooking class, a project at work, a new computer program, or an upcoming family reunion, they're excited about some element of their life. It can be a big thing or a little thing. It can be a brand new car or brand new buds on the crepe myrtle bush. It can be a vacation home or a new tool for the workbench. It can be making a cake or making a difference. It can be having lunch with a friend or enjoying a cup of tea by yourself. It can be teaching a puppy a new trick or teaching an "old dog" a new skill.

Again, it doesn't matter what it is. The point is finding that "something" that turns you on, that gets you going, and that makes you say "I'm excited about this. This is interesting, challenging, stimulating, fun." Having enthusiasm gives us a reason to get up in the morning and the motivation to keep going once we're up.

Ask yourself the question, "What am I excited about today?" Find something that causes you to be enthusiastic. It's the fuel for having great days and for making life count.

38

Invest Wisely.

*"Do not store up for yourselves treasure on
earth,where moth and rust destroy,
and where thieves break in and steal.
But lay up for yourselves treasure in heaven,
where moth and rust do not destroy, and
where thieves do not break in and steal.
For where your treasure is,
there your heart will be also."*
Matthew 6:19-21

I n the past few years, people have been talking about and focusing on their investments. The unprecedented success of the stock market has prompted everyone from tycoons to teenagers to become interested in investing. Whether people are working with registered brokers or day-trading on the Internet, investing is a hot topic.

When we think about investing, we generally think in terms of money. It's the asset that first comes to mind. But in truth, we have three resources that we can invest. And we have *only* three. The resources that we have are our money, our time, and our energy. Each one is valuable and is limited, so investing wisely becomes paramount to our happiness and wellbeing.

I had just finished speaking at an event for a large hospital system when a tall, well-spoken woman came up to talk with me. She told me that she had worked at the hospital for almost twenty years and that she had worked all those years so that she could invest. That piqued my interest.

"Invest in what?" I asked, thinking that she might have a hot mutual fund to recommend.

"Well," she said, "some people invest in the stock market, but I decided a long time ago that I would invest in my children. I invested my money in their education and my time and energy in making them responsible people. I knew," she said, "that it would be a wise investment that would pay off for all of us. And it has." She proudly told me that her children turned out well. They are doctors and lawyers and are contributing citizens who have made their mother – and society – rich.

At the beginning of the twentieth century, American financier J.P. Morgan was a multimillionaire. As the head of a powerful international banking firm, Morgan made a fortune investing in railroads and steel mills. He was a captain of industry and was so financially influential that he literally held the economy of the United States in the palm of his hand.

Although Morgan was a tough, hard-driving businessman, he had a soft side. He adored his children and was extremely proud of them. In fact, he once commented to his father, "I only wish all my investments would turn out as well." In spite of his wealth, he realized that life's real pay-off comes from investing in the things that are really important, not just in stocks and bonds.

Where are you investing your three resources? All you have is your money, your time, and your energy. Are you investing them in places that will pay off for you, that will give you the kind of riches and rewards that you want? All the money in the world can't make up for wasted time or energy spent on things that don't really matter.

My mother often said that what you have on the outside isn't nearly as valuable as what you have on the inside. The woman at the hospital understood that concept. By investing in her children and their future, she was successful in ways that many Wall Street investors would envy.

Your resources are limited. So invest wisely, and make life count.

39

Keep on
Keepin' On.

"Never, never, never, never give up."
Winston Churchill

*"Don't look back –
something might be gaining on you."*
Satchel Paige

*"Success is measured not so much
by the position one has attained in life,
but by the obstacles he or she has overcome
while trying to succeed."*
Booker T. Washington

*"Many of life's failures are men who did not
realize how close they were to success
when they gave up."*
Thomas Edison

"Victory belongs to the most persevering."
Napoleon

*"Adversity causes some men to break,
others to break records."*
William A. Ward

"It's always too soon to quit."
Norman Vincent Peale

I have such admiration for those tenacious, determined, focused people who know what they want and absolutely refuse to let anything get in the way of their accomplishing it. It's been my experience that the thing that usually prevents us from getting what we want is ourselves. We give up too easily. Instead of "quitting while we're ahead," we quit before we ever get ahead, sometimes before we even get started.

Sometimes we are challenged by the experiences of life. We've all had things happen in our lives that we didn't choose or that we didn't plan. No one plans on divorce, illness, death of loved ones, job lose, disability, but nonetheless, those things occur, and perhaps it is in those circumstances when we are challenged to "keep on keepin' on."

How do you keep going? How do you keep at the task at hand when you're feeling overwhelmed?

First, admit that you can't do it alone. Give your situation up to God. Trust in Him for guidance and strength. And turn, too, to friends, family, and wise counselors for help. No one person has all the answers, and especially in the challenging times, we need the advice and the assistance of others.

Second, remember that you're a lot stronger and tougher than you think you are. We human beings have a tremendous capacity for courage and strength. People who have gone through great difficulty often look back in amazement at how successfully they survived, and even prospered. during those trials. In the difficult times, people discover that they have untapped resources of skills and stamina.

Third, we "keep on keepin' on" by sheer determination and the realization that through our efforts, we can succeed. We can be successful either in reaching our objectives or in surviving a tough situation. Remember Churchill's words, *"Never, never, never, never give up."*

Make Life Count!

40

Let Go.

*"The most difficult thing for people to say
in twenty-five words or less is good-bye."*
Unknown

*"It's not an empty nest until
they get their stuff out of the basement."*
On a T-shirt

"It's all in the letting go."
Shirley Garrett

There are so many times in life when we need to let go. Letting go isn't easy. It's often painful and scary.

From the time that we begin to understand the sequence of life, we know that someday we'll have to let our parents go. From the day our children are born, we know that eventually we'll have to let them go.

Sometimes we choose to let go of relationships or jobs, but at other times, circumstances beyond our control make those choices for us. We are often forced out of our comfort zones, and we have to let go of our expectations and our dreams.

Some of our "letting go" experiences are difficult and painful and scary, but in some cases, letting go can be freeing. In the letting go, we free ourselves to be open to new relationships, new opportunities, new adventures, and new dreams. By letting go, we expand our horizons and grow in ways we never knew we could.

Letting go requires courage, the courage to take the leap, to step out into unknown territory. Ray Bradbury said, "First you jump off the cliff, and you build your wings on the way down." There is exhilaration in taking that step and in building your wings.

Do you need to let go of some things in your life? Do you need to say good-bye to some old habits? Do you need to break out of some old patterns in order to build new and different patterns of behavior?

Think about who you are and who you want to be. Think about where you are and where you want to go. And if you decide that there are some things that need to change, have courage. Jump off the cliff. Let go, build your wings, and have a great day.

41

Be Generous.

"Each man should give what he has
decided in his heart to give,
not reluctantly or under compulsion,
for God loves a cheerful giver."
2 Corinthians 10:7

"No person was ever honored
for what he received.
Honors have always been
awards for what people give."
Calvin Coolidge

"You give but little when you give possessions;
it is when you give of yourself
that you truly give."
Kahlil Gibran

"And do not forget to do good
and to share with others,
for with such sacrifices God is pleased."
Hebrews 13:16

"Earn all you can, save all you can,
give all you can."
John Wesley

"A generous man will prosper;
he who refreshes others
will himself be refreshed."
Proverbs 11:25

P eople who have great days are generous. To be generous is to give magnanimously, unselfishly, liberally. It is a sharing of one's gifts.

We discussed in an earlier chapter that we human beings have only three assets: our time, our energy, and our money. Just as these assets need to be invested wisely in the important areas of our life, we should be generous in the giving of these assets as well.

Being generous is the right thing to do, and it is also the wise thing to do. It seems that people who give freely reap great personal rewards. The personal satisfaction that they get from spending time with someone in need, expending energy as a volunteer, or giving money to a worthy cause is a rich benefit. Knowing that they're sharing their blessings pays off for them in a variety of ways. And they know that generosity begets generosity.

A woman told me that she and a group of her senior citizen friends meet at a local restaurant for breakfast one morning a week. They're "regulars" at the restaurant. They always sit at the same table, and they always have the same waitress, a young woman who has become more than a waitress; she's a friend.

One morning the waitress was very excited. An earlier customer had left her a tip of $100! She was stunned when she discovered the tip, and feeling sure that the customer had made a mistake, she had run after him. "No mistake," the customer said. "You did a good job. I want you to have the hundred dollars."

When her "regulars" arrived and took their places at the table, the waitress shared with them the story of the tip. But she shared more than the story. She proved that generosity begets generosity. She bought breakfast for them!

How generous are you? Do you give as much as you are able of your time, your energy, and your money? When good things happen to you, when you're the beneficiary of someone's generosity, do you share it with others? Try it. You'll be surprised how good you'll feel, and you may be surprised by the generosity that comes back to you in unexpected ways. Be generous...and have a great day.

Make Life Count!

42

Hug.

"It's wondrous what a hug can do,
A hug can cheer you when you're blue;
A hug can say, 'I love you so,'
Or, 'Gee, I hate to let you go.'
...So stretch those arms without delay
And give someone a hug today."
Unknown

"When certain people hug you, it fills up
your heart a certain number of spaces."
Zeke Lee Garrett, age 9

I love hugs. A hug is warmer than a fur coat and more comforting than a cashmere sweater.

Give someone a hug. You might begin by hugging yourself. Just wrap your arms around yourself, and give yourself a hug. You deserve it.

Now, hug someone else. Hug your spouse, your children, your grandchildren. Hug your siblings, your aunts, your uncles, your cousins, your grandparents. Hug your pet. Hug your in-laws. Hug a child, an elderly person, your friends. Hug everyone you care about.

A hug shares the warmth of human affection. So hug someone today.

43
Ask.

"Ask, and it will be given;
seek, and you will find;
knock, and the door will be opened to you."
Luke 11:9

"...you do not have because you do not ask."
James 4:2

"You don't always get what you ask for,
but you never get what you don't ask for –
unless it's contagious!"
Franklyn Bronde

"The most you'll ever get is what you ask for."
Unknown

Most of us were brought up to be self-reliant. We were taught to be strong, independent, and self-sufficient. Some of us were taught that asking for help was intrusive on others or a sign of weakness, laziness, or helplessness.

While I'm a great believer in personal responsibility, I'm also convinced that there are times when we need to ask for what we need or want. We need to ask for help, information, counsel, business, feedback, attention, affection, referrals – whatever it is that we're seeking. And then we must be willing to give back when the same is asked of us.

Sometimes the circumstances of life force us into asking. A number of years ago, as a young mother with two little boys, ages five and fourteen months, I was compelled by a short-term physical disability to be totally dependent on the assistance of others. I developed carpal tunnel syndrome. The carpal tunnel is the passage in the wrist through which the nerves and blood vessels pass. For some still undetermined reason, those tunnels in both my wrists began to constrict. I would wake up each morning with both arms numb. Normal activities, such as drying my hair, dressing, cleaning house, and caring for my children, became increasingly challenging.

At first, the doctor recommended medication and immobilizing the wrists with splints, and while these methods helped alleviate some of the symptoms, they didn't solve the problem. The only solution was surgery, surgery on both hands at the same time!

Can you imagine it? Following the procedure, I was totally dependent on other people for my basic needs. I could do nothing for myself that involved using my hands. I couldn't care for my children. I couldn't make a phone call. I couldn't write or type. I couldn't open a door or a drawer. I couldn't bathe myself, dress myself, feed myself, brush my teeth, comb my hair, or even go to the bathroom by myself. For the first time in my life, I had to ask for help with even the simplest of tasks. And fortunately, help was available. My husband, my mother, my mother-in-law, and close friends were there to help me get through a difficult time.

I learned a lot from that experience. I learned that the ability to take care of one-self is a gift and that independence is something to be appreciated. I got a sampling of what it must be like to be disabled. I knew my disability was short-termed, but I developed empathy for those who face those challenges for a lifetime. I learned that no matter how determined or stubborn or self-reliant one is, – and I am all those things – there may come a time when one has to depend on others, a time when we have to ask for help.

You've no doubt heard it said that the reason Moses wandered in the desert for forty years was because, like most men, he refused to ask for directions! I can relate to Moses. I don't like asking for help either, so I often hesitate to ask.

I hesitate to ask, because I don't want to bother people or intrude on their time, and yet, I've discovered that people are usually very willing to give assistance and, in truth, are often flattered by being asked.

I hesitate to ask, because I don't want to appear ignorant. I don't want people to know that I don't have all the answers when it comes to my finances, or my car, or my computer, or all the other things in this complicated world that I don't understand.

And yet, I'm learning that, as Will Rogers said, "Every man (and woman) is ignorant... just on different subjects." No one is good at everything. Consequently, in our areas of strength, we should be willing to share, and in our areas of weakness, we should be willing to ask.

Although I hesitate to ask, I'm working on not being so hesitant. I'm realizing that when we ask for help we give others an opportunity to be the experts, to share information, to give us assistance, to show us the way. When we ask, we shine the spotlight on the capabilities of others. And when we ask with an attitude of appreciation, in a manner that is gracious and not demanding, we find the help we need and at the same time, create the opportunity to give back.

Ask, seek, find...and have a great day.

44

Hope.

"Hope sees the invisible, feels the intangible, and achieves the impossible."
Unknown

"Hope deferred makes the heart sick, but a longing fulfilled is a tree of life."
Proverbs 13:12

People who have great days are those who are hopeful. They have positive expectations about the future, and they hold on to those expectations even when present circumstances are bleak.

One of my favorite movies is *The Shawshank Redemption.* An Academy Award winner from several years ago, the movie focuses on the inmates of the Shawshank penitentiary. Because of its subject matter, it's a tough movie to watch. Its violence and language paint a grim picture of prison life. But, surprisingly, the theme of the movie is hope. Hope is the thing that gives the protagonist, Andy Dufresne, not only the will to keep going but also the desire to create hope in his fellow inmates. Andy inspires them to find purpose, to seek knowledge, to cultivate friendships, to see beauty, and to even find humor in the worst of circumstances. Andy teaches his best friend, Red, that hope is a good thing, maybe the best of things, and that no good thing ever dies.

Motivated by his hope and fueled by his determination, Andy Dufresne uses his intellect to miraculously escape from the prison. Sometime later, Red, who before meeting Andy had given up hope and had expected to spend the rest of his life in prison, is released. As he begins a search to locate his friend, Red says to himself, "I hope I make it across the border. I hope I see my friend. I hope the Pacific is as blue as it's been in my dreams. I hope..." Through Andy, he found hope where none had been before.

Hope is what it's all about. No matter what, never lose hope – that positive expectation of the future. Hope...and have a great day.

45

Celebrate Your Uniqueness.

*"You can be the ordinary thread in the tunic,
or you can be the purple, that touch of brilliance
that gives distinction to the rest."*
Epictetus

*"Always be a first-rate version of yourself
instead of a second-rate version
of someone else."*
Judy Garland

"Be distinct, or you'll be extinct."
Tom Peters

"You are unique...just like everyone else."
Unknown

*"Nobody can be exactly like me.
Sometimes even I have trouble doing it."*
Tallulah Bankhead

What is your uniqueness? What is it that makes you different? What is it that sets you apart from others? Each of us is unique, a special creation of God.

While we share many similarities, we are distinctive because of our differences. We each possess a special combination of characteristics, talents, and aptitudes that make us different from every other human being on the face of the earth.

Much of our uniqueness is inborn. No other human being has fingerprints like mine. No one else shares your DNA, not even your siblings. No one else's irises match yours. No other voice is exactly the same as mine. What a miracle to be unique!

"Branding" is a hot topic in marketing today. Businesses want to be recognized by their distinctive brand. They want their logo, their colors, and their slogans to establish an identity for them in the marketplace. They want their products and services to stand out from the crowd, to be recognized as unique.

Today, consider the characteristics of your own personal "brand." Think about the things that make you stand out from the crowd. Consider how very special you are. Consider the brilliant combination of traits and gifts that make you YOU. Consider how you're using your uniqueness to live your life with your own special style. Celebrate your uniqueness, and make it count.

46

Appreciate Your Friends.

"Make new friends, but keep the old;
One is silver, and the other, gold."
Camp song

"Little friends may prove great friends."
Aesop

"It's the friends that you can call up
at four a.m. that matter."
Marlene Dietrich

"A friend is someone who knows you
better than you know yourself
and loves you in spite of it."
Proverb

Your friends are those cherished folks with whom you can laugh, cry, and be yourself. With them you can be silly or serious; with them you can share adventures and experiences; with them you can share your deepest thoughts and your wildest dreams. Along with your family, your friends are the characters in the story of your life.

Friends are the people who are there for you in the good times and the bad. They are there to dance with you at your wedding and at the weddings of your children and grand-children. And they are there to cry with you at the funerals of your loved ones.

Friends are those who know you at your best and at your worst. They share your suc-cesses and your failures, your triumphs and your tragedies. They're with you on the mountaintop and at rock bottom. They've seen you without make-up and without the mask you wear for the world. They've seen you when your eyes are red and swollen from tears and when your eyes are filled with tears of joy, and at all these times, they love you as you are.

They listen when you pour out your heart and support you when you share your dreams. They hold you accountable, and they hold your hand to help you get back on track when you've lost your way. They keep your secrets, keep you going, and keep you in their prayers.

Right now, stop and call a friend. Tell that person how much you love them and appre-ciate them. Tell that friend how grateful you are to have them in your life. Appreciate your friends, and have a great day.

Be Responsible.

*"Man's self concept is enhanced
when he takes responsibility for himself."*
Will Schutz

*"Remember the three R's:
Respect for self.
Respect for others.
Responsibility for all your actions."*
Unknown

*"The best parachute folders
are those who jump themselves."*
Unknown

"The price of greatness is responsibility."
Winston Churchill

People who have great days are those who take responsibility for their decisions and their actions. They realize that they are responsible for the choices they make.

We live in a blaming world. When things go wrong, we want to blame the media, the traffic, the weather, the economy, the Democrats, or the Republicans. We blame God. We blame the Baptists, the Catholics, the Jews, the Presbyterians, the Muslims. We blame the boss, company policy, our co-workers, or our competitors. We blame the churches, the schools, the government, the insurance companies, the stock market. We blame our genes, our hormones, our metabolism, our biorhythms, our horoscope. We blame our parents, our spouses, our ex-spouses, our children, our stepchildren, our in-laws, our neighbors. While we make a habit of blaming others for the things we don't like, we're reluctant to take responsibility for our contribution to the problem.

If you want more great days, become more responsible. Take responsibility for your choices, your decisions, your thoughts, and your actions. When you become responsible, you have a sense of control. You no longer see yourself as a victim.

Yes, there are lots of things over which you and I have absolutely no control. But in those cases, while we can't control the circumstances or events, we can control our response to them. "Response-ability" is our ability to respond, and we have the choice as to how we react to every circumstance that comes our way.

Do you want to have more great days? Do you want to make life count? Start by being responsible.

48

Be Your Best Self.

*"The key is not to try to be a
Mozart or an Einstein. Rather it is to be a far
more productive version of yourself. Once you
have identified a mission that calls you to
action, you can train yourself in the skills
to succeed in it."*
Charles Garfield

*"Make the most of what you have;
be the best that you can be."*
Julie Alexander

*"If you wish to be like someone else,
you waste the person you are."*
Unknown

"Whatever you are, be a good one."
Abraham Lincoln

*"Most women are not as young
as they are painted."*
Sir Max Beerbohm

"Only the mediocre are always at their best."
Jean Giradeux

I n one of my favorite "Dennis the Menace"
cartoons, Dennis says to Joey, "The very
best thing that you can do is to get very

good at being you!" There's a lot of wisdom in those words.

Each of us is unique. Each one has his or her special gifts and talents. We're not all good at everything, but we're all good at something.

Whether it's our appearance, our intellect, our talents, our career, our level of physical fitness, or our relationships, we should all be about the business of improving, of constantly getting better at what we do and being our best selves. Why just "get by" when you could be "getting better."

Perhaps our mission should be to discover the best that is within us and to work to make it better. When you "get very good at being you," when you are the best that you can be, you fulfill your purpose on this earth. That's when you make life count and have great days.

49

Be Grateful.

*"There is a calmness to life lived in gratitude,
a quiet joy."*
Ralph H. Blum

"Praise God from whom all blessings flow."
The Doxology

"Celebrate Thanksgiving every single day."
Julie Alexander

To truly have a life full of great days, one must be grateful. We must have an attitude of appreciation for the blessings that we have.

What are you grateful for today? Here are a few things to consider:

- If you can see, hear, touch, smell, or taste, you're having a great day.

- If you have a roof over your head, you're having a great day.

- If you have a bed, you're having a great day.

- If you have access to a clean bathroom and a hot shower, you're having a great day.

- If you have food on your table, you're having a great day.

- If you have something to wear, you're having a great day.

- If you have a pair of shoes, you're having a great day.

- If you have at least one person who loves you, you're having a great day.

- If you have at least one person to love, you're having a great day.

- If you can read and write, you're having a great day.

- If you have electricity and running water, you're having a great day.

- If you want or need a job, and you have one, you're having a great day.

- If you can get out of bed in the morning, you're having a great day.

- If you have at least one really good friend, you're having a great day.

- If you can find something to laugh about, you're having a great day.

- If you can see a tree, you're having a great day.

- If you can get from one place to another, you're having a great day.

- If you have health insurance and don't need it today, you're having a great day.

- If you can walk, you're having a great day.

- If you can talk, you're having a great day.

- If you can help someone, you're having a great day.

- If you have a little money in your pocket, you're having a great day.

- If you have something to look forward to, you're having a great day.

- If you've smiled today, you're having a great day.

- If someone has smiled at you, you're having a great day.

- If you have something to do, you're having a great day.

So, what are you grateful for today?

Here's a suggestion. Every day list 3-5 things for which you're grateful. Some days it'll be easy to think of lots of things that you're thankful for, but truthfully, there may be other days when listing even one or two may be a struggle.

But every day, pay attention to the things in your life that are reasons for gratitude. Keep a running list, and on those days when you're feeling down in the dumps, when nothing seems to be going your way, when you're hurt or disappointed, when it seems as if the whole world has turned against you, read through your gratitude list and be reminded of how blessed you really are.

Start your list right now...and have a grateful day.

50

Make Life Count! It's Up to You.

*"Everything has been figured out
except how to live."*
Jean-Paul Sartre

*"So oftentimes it happens
that we live our lives in chains,
That we never even know we have the key."*
The Eagles

"And that's the way it is."
Walter Cronkite

So, how do you make life count? How do you have great days? It's not a deep, dark secret; it's not rocket science; there's no magic formula. If you want more great days, you can have them. It's up to you. You do, indeed, hold the key.

One of my favorite characters of American cultural history is Anna Mary Robertson Moses. Better known as "Grandma Moses," this spunky, self-reliant woman became a legend in her own time. A farm wife from upstate New York, Grandma Moses didn't even begin her career until she was in her eighties. Nonetheless, she became not only a recognized artist but also, and perhaps more importantly, a symbol of life and hope and vitality.

Anna Mary Robertson married Thomas Moses in the fall of 1887. As a young wife and mother, she endured the many challenges of farm life – failed crops, long days, hard work, little income, and few comforts. Anna Mary had ten children, but only five survived. One was stillborn and four others died from the diseases that claimed the lives of many children of that era.

To make ends meet, she started several businesses. She raised cows and made and sold butter from their milk; she made and sold potato chips; she raised chickens, and she always had a little money stashed away for emergencies. A capable businesswoman, she managed her finances well. In fact, she said, "Whenever Thomas borrowed money from me, as he sometimes did, I always kept it legal. I wrote up a little note and charged him interest!"

Her love of art began in childhood. Her father encouraged her creativity by giving her large sheets of white paper, and she would paint pictures using the juice of grapes and other berries for color. Paper wasn't always available, so she painted pictures on anything she could find – pieces of wood, slate, and even windowpanes.

After childhood, her painting was done out of necessity. When there was no money for wallpaper, Grandma Moses put white paper on the walls and decorated it with painted landscapes. It was after her husband died that she began painting pictures for gifts and "just for fun."

In the late 1940's, when Grandma Moses was an octogenarian, a prominent New York art collector discovered her work, and Grandma Moses became a national figure, a celebrity. She was interviewed by *Life* magazine and interviewed on the radio. She visited the White House and had tea with President and Mrs. Truman. Truman even played the piano for her.

Grandma Moses died at the age of 101, but the story of her life lives on in her autobiography. In this book, she shared not only her life story but also her philosophy. The conclusion of the book reads:

"I have written my life in small sketches, a little today, a little yesterday – remembering the good days and the unpleasant ones – because that is how they come, and that is how we have to take them. I was happy and contented and made the best of what life had to offer. And life is what we make it, always has been, always will be."

There it is – the way to make life count and to have great days. As Grandma Moses said, there are good days and bad ones. That's how they come, and that's how we have to take them. She made the best of what life had to offer. And she understood that life is what we make it, always has been, always will be.

Whether or not you have great days is up to you. If you want to have more great days, you can have them. If you want your life to count, you can make it happen.

Follow Grandma Moses' advice. Make the best of what life has to offer. Life is what we make it, so make life count!

Order Form

of copies

_____ **Make Life Count! 50 Ways to Great Days**

_____ **Great Days: 50 Ways to Add Energy, Enthusiasm, & Enjoyment to Your Life**

_____ **Total copies**

Please send $11.95 per book
+ $2.55 shipping and handling.

Make checks payable to
Great Days Presentations

Name _____

Address _____

City _____ State _____ Zip _____

Phone _____

E-mail _____

Your books will be autographed. If you'd like a personalized inscription on gift copies, please include the name of each recipient with your order.

Great Days Presentations
2002 Shari Lane
Garland, TX 75043
toll free (877) 478-3297
info@www.JulieAlexander.com